Bad Language in Business

www.southbankpublishing.com

'A man thinks that by mouthing hard words he understands hard things.'

Herman Melville

Bad Language in Business

Graham Edmonds

southbank
publishing

First published in 2008 by Southbank Publishing,
21 Great Ormond Street, London WC1N 3JB

www.southbankpublishing.com

A CIP catalogue record for this book is available from the British Library.

ISBN 978-1-904915-35-5

2 4 6 8 10 9 7 5 3 1

Typeset by Avocet Typeset, Chilton, Aylesbury, Bucks
Printed and bound in Great Britain by CPD, Blaina, Wales

Contents

5

CONTENTS

Introduction

By using the title *Bad Language in Business* I'm not referring to swearing, cussing or cursing (although I do cover
their usage) but at the way we use words to manipulate,
prevaricate and generally to communicate our aims and
needs while conducting our work. This book looks at the
relationship that the business world has with the English
language and how it is used, abused and altered for advantage.

Whatever the situation – a presentation, sales patter, business propaganda, making a speech, a negotiation or a
simple meeting – the purpose of this book is to help you
decipher and avoid some of the common linguistic annoy-
ances commonly found in business life.

Corporate language should be clear and to the point, but in
reality it often hides behind meaningless words and phrases
that are designed to make the user sound clever or credible.
Much of the content of this book has become synonymous
with bad language in business and its widespread use has
led to a culture of mistrust in the corporate world, especially for those outside it. Credibility is a vital component

in being successful in business and the way you use language is critical to the way you are perceived, the way you maintain your business relationships and how you build on those throughout your business life.

1

Bad Language

'Swearing is like any other music… If it is not done well, if it is not done with a fine and discriminating art, and vitalized with gracious and heartborn feeling, it lacks beauty, it lacks charm, it lacks expression, it lacks nobleness, it lacks majesty…'

David Gridley

Swearwords are classed under the heading 'bad language', but it turns out swearing is not all that bad. According to some research conducted by the University of East Anglia, it may actually be good for team morale: using swearwords keeps stress down and helps with team bonding.

Professor Yehuda Baruch, who carried out the research, warned that attempts to prevent workers from swearing could have a negative impact:

> In most scenarios, in particular in the presence of customers or senior staff, profanity must be seriously discouraged or banned. However, our study suggested that, in many cases, taboo language serves the needs of people for developing and maintaining solidarity, and as a mechanism to cope with stress. Banning it could backfire. The challenge is to master the art of knowing when to turn a blind eye to communication that does not meet with the manager's own standards.

It's clear that a good manager must be able to understand what levels of swearing are acceptable to his or her team and adjust their language accordingly. And it may seem obvious, but swearing in front of your customers is never a good idea.

It may be worth first exploring which swear words are generally acceptable. The BBC has apparently ranked the most common swearwords according to their level of offensiveness. Following is my list, which adds a few to theirs.

The following 'acceptable' words are not necessarily classed as swearwords in the accepted sense, but are replacements for other gutsier, generally unacceptable ones…

Balls
Blooming
Bottom
BS
Bum
Crud
Darn
Dreck
Effing
Flipping
Fudge
Heck
Pardon my French
P'd
Screwed
Shoot
Sugar

The following are deemed just about acceptable. Often these words are changed or added to in some way, for example buggeration.

Arse
Arsehole
Balls-up
Bloody
Bugger
Bullshit
Cock-up
Crap

Crikey
Damn
Dickhead
Fart
Feck
Frigging
Knob
Manure
Plonker
Ruddy
Shoot
Sodding
Tits
Turd
Twat

These words begin to push the boundaries:

Bollocks (acceptability varies enormously)
Cock
Cow
Piss
Prick
Shag
Shit
Slag
Wank or Wanker
Whore

Any of the preceding may be accompanied by the bizarre 'pardon my French'.

The following are considered unacceptable: using one of

these is considered 'going too far' in most societies and workplaces.

Bastard
Cunt
Motherfucker
Paedo

Insult avoidance techniques include acronyms such as these:

FNG – Fucking New Guy
FOFO – Fuck Off and Find Out
FRO – Fuck Right Off
FUBB – Fucked Up Beyond Belief
FUF – Fuck Up Factor

Of course, these can be annoying in other ways too, but as an aside, I once worked with a manager whose favourite little insult was to nod at his victim and with a smile say, 'C U Next Tuesday.'

In recent years the term 'swearword' has also come to cover any racist or defamatory religious term, so in the 'completely unacceptable' category we must include terms and names such as Paki, nigger, Jesus Christ and Jew, and their various connotations and variations.

Terms like spastic, spaz or any derogatory term relating to the disabled and mentally ill are universally considered to be totally unacceptable. England football manager Glenn Hoddle lost his job for saying the following in an interview to the *Sunday Times*...

You and I have been physically given two hands and two legs and half-decent brains. Some people have not been born like that for a reason. The karma is working from another lifetime. I have nothing to hide about that. It is not only people with disabilities. What you sow, you have to reap.

However, you can go too far in trying to be too politically correct. In the summer of 2008 it was reported that one local government in England has instructed employees to use the term 'thought showers' in the place of 'brainstorming'. Tunbridge Wells Borough Council in Kent stated that memos have been sent to workers instructing them not to say 'brainstorming' because it may offend epileptics or the mentally ill. When asked, charities involved said there was no need for a ban. Richard Colwill of the mental health charity SANE said, 'This ban goes too far. Few would be genuinely offended by the word brainstorming in the context of council meetings.'

Recently a Radio 1 DJ substituted the word gay for rubbish when describing a ring-tone, and the BBC Board of Governors defended his actions by saying the word gay 'was often now used to mean "lame" or "rubbish"' and that 'this is a widespread current usage... among young people'. Whatever you think of the use and context of the word, it's another example of how English can rapidly develop: an apparently harmless word originally meaning 'merry' has been quickly metamorphosed into an insult.

The world of television can reflect and influence business. First, here's an example of that and how adaptable the language is.

The makers of the TV show *Father Ted* knew that they couldn't use the 'f-word' on Irish TV, so they adapted the word feck (original meaning to throw or to steal) and that has become a more-or-less acceptable substitute for the unacceptable. It works better on every level; for example 'you little fecker' is less offensive than 'you little fucker', you can even smile as you say it. In the US it's common to use the word freak in a similar way to feck, while in the hit TV series *Battlestar Gallactica* they use frak as a substitute. Everyone knows what they mean but somehow it now becomes acceptable on prime-time TV. Recently a computer engineer came to my office to fix a PC, and when his repair went wrong he actually said 'frak it'. He told me it was in common usage within his peer group.

Many managers tend to swear out of frustration at themselves and at their lack of ability to control a given situation. Extreme in this style is Malcolm Tucker, a fictional spin-doctor character in the political sitcom *The Thick of It*. Famous for his bullying, his streams of invective and his creativity (possibly his most famous phrase came when someone knocked at his office door – 'Come the fuck in or fuck the fuck off'), we watch as his character veers between oath-spattered highs of success and lows of despair. Like many real-life aggressive managers you have to wonder whether he would be as effective if he was unable to swear.

Weak managers use aggression and swearing to disguise their faults. Tucker and managers like him often get away with swearing simply by sheer force of personality or because it's so ingrained in their character make-up.

A good example of this type of boss is the chef Gordon

Ramsay, who curses his way through his TV shows. Underneath all that guff and hot-air, he is undoubtedly a superb manager and motivator, although some would say that his style borders on bullying. His audience generally accept him and his swearing because of his successful track record and his victims seem to deserve his wrath... at least that's the impression we get from the way the series is edited. Ramsey's hot and cold style is necessary for good television and that doesn't make it acceptable for most work places.

There are people who don't watch Ramsay's TV shows precisely because he swears so much; this especially applies to the generation that were in their prime in the 1950s and 1960s. Watching veteran 80-year-old entertainer Bruce Forsyth being interviewed on the *Friday Night with Jonathan Ross* show, almost the first thing he did was to tell Ross not to swear because (and that whole generation would probably say this) 'it's not necessary'.

In a business setting, why take the risk of upsetting a significant minority of your audience by swearing?

2

Audience

'Make sure you have finished speaking
before your audience has finished
listening…'

Dorothy Sarnoff

Here's a good illustration of how confused a situation can become when audience perceptions change and why it's so difficult dealing with issues such as religion, race and sex. This comes from a speech made by the late Charlton Heston to the Harvard Law School in 1999:

> But when I told an audience last year that white pride is just as valid as black pride or red pride or anyone else's pride, they called me a racist. I've worked with brilliantly talented homosexuals all my life. But when I told an audience that gay rights should extend no further than your rights or my rights, I was called a homophobe. I served in World War Two against the Axis powers. But during a speech, when I drew an analogy between singling out innocent Jews and singling out innocent gun owners, I was called an anti-Semite. Everyone I know knows I would never raise a closed fist against my country. But when I asked an audience to oppose this cultural persecution, I was compared to Timothy McVeigh.

Whatever your own views about Heston it illustrates the point that, in business, companies must give their managers clear guidance when it comes to sensitive topics. The reality is that it's all about the audience and what they want to hear. The strength of the message can be controlled and language skills are an integral part of that.

In this case, it's a fair bet to assume that the majority of Heston's audience during this speech was white and middle class. A champion of equal rights, he often spoke out about what he saw as racism against 'white, hard-working, NRA card-carrying Americans'. His view was that everyone had the same rights no matter whether they were gay, black, white, disabled or tattooed sky-blue; there should be no special cases.

You can almost hear the anger in his words and no doubt with his acting skills he could add to its effectiveness by reinforcing his message using body language and tone of voice.

Controversy only occurs when there is a misunderstanding between parties; usually one misinterpreting the other or one side deliberately taking a stance to provoke a response.

The language used can drastically alter the way something is interpreted, as can the medium or mechanism in which it's delivered, whether by email, letter, telephone, face-to-face conversation or by formal presentation. It can inflame the situation or cool it, depending on how it is presented and then interpreted.

To be effective in imparting a message and to get the required response, it is essential that the deliverer be aware of their audience and its general agenda or views.

Newspapers provide a very good example; they know their readers and how to provoke a response which in turn will lead to better sales. Generally, when it comes to subjects that sell, in the UK it goes like this:

Broadsheet newspapers – the biggest news event of the day, the economy, house prices, the environment, the arts, sport, health, education and business

Mid-market tabloids – showbiz, sport, celebrities, TV, health, the royal family, terrorism, house prices and education, (anti) Europe

Red top tabloids – sport, sex, celebrities, TV, the royal family, human interest, horoscopes, top news story overview

Let's take a typical story and compare how the language and headlines change according to the audience. In spring 2008 an easterly wind blew across England; this is an unusual event as the predominant winds are mainly westerly. It brought with it a smell, described as 'sulphurous' or 'farmyard'. The Met Office attributed the odour to industrial or agricultural pollution from mainland Europe.

The newspaper headlines ran...

Guardian – 'What's that Smell? A Whiff of Europe'

Daily Mail – 'Der Stink: Germany to blame for terrible smell engulfing England blown in by freak weather' (this was changed from Le Stink as originally they thought the smell came from France)

Sun – 'German Hogs "Pong for Europe"' (the Eurovision Song Contest is often referred to as A Song for Europe)

Both the *Sun* and the *Mail* also mentioned that 'not even the Queen was immune at home in Windsor Castle', as if she lives her life smelling only nice things. The *Guardian*'s story accurately explained the reasons for the smell but

23

couldn't resist having a pop at the *Mail* and its apparent xenophobia.

It's this basic dislike and distrust that many English people have of those living in mainland Europe that both the *Sun* and the *Mail* play on and exploit to sell their papers – it makes the British reader feel superior so more likely to buy the paper.

The *Guardian*, meanwhile, plays on the fact that its readers like to feel more enlightened and superior to the readers of the tabloids. Its article also helpfully reported on the National Farmer's Union comments, which reflected another agenda:

> This is what happens when farmers are forced to empty their slurry store all in one go at the same time instead of being able to apply it little and often during the winter. We are grateful to the Dutch farmers for laying on such a pungent demonstration of what could happen every spring here in the UK if the government presses ahead with its ill-conceived proposal to implement a blanket ban on winter slurry spreading.

You can find many applications for this agenda and audience-driven approach in business. This is especially true when it comes to financial reports or year-end statements or results, when the aim is to deflect attention away from potential problems. Emphasis is placed on good news and creating what's usually described as a *feel good factor* about the company in question. In this case, the audience are the investors, shareholders and media whose comments can affect the share price.

Clichés that can indicate that not all is well include:

Back to basics – you're meant to think that this represents a return to a fundamental and uncomplicated way of doing something. Many companies say this when they've gone through a period of unsuccessful diversification or when a new leader arrives and wants to make changes. Also look out for *keep it simple, grass roots and root and branch*.

Core or non-core – this is referring to activities that the company in question should be doing and where they should have known better. Terms like *stick to the knitting* usually accompany this.

Consumer or customer focused – this means they want to be able to learn more about customers so that they can sell more products. It works but it's not usually good news for the customer. Look out for *client focused, customer obsessed, consumer intuitive, connect with the customer* and that old favourite *empathy*.

Exceptional – usually referring to a one-off event such as a large write-down or something that affects sales, or normal but unforeseeable costs that the management wishes to present as unrepeatable. In fact, something exceptional happens every year.

Laying the foundations – a euphemism for 'let's just forget about this year's bad performance and concentrate on next year's potentially good showing'. Also watch out for *looking to the future and future facing*.

Re-engineer – a term meaning to change, it has sinister overtones as its use is generally associated with job losses. Alternatives include *reinventing and step change*.

Shareholder value – creating money for shareholders is the aim of nearly every company; to have to mention it is a sure sign of insecurity.

Sub-optimal – business speak for below standard.

Systemic – usually used as part of a *blame game*; i.e. 'It's not me, guv, it's the system.'

Transparency, greater visibility, openness – a promise to be open, with nothing hidden; usually to do with not hiding company results with spin or PR bullshit, and if you believe that then you'll believe anything.

If the company in question wants to be vague, then the usual technique is to waffle about strategy, including the usual *mission* or *vision statements*. Strategies come in several forms:

Strategic direction – where they think we're going
Strategic approach – how they think they're going to go about it
Strategic fit – those who are going with them
Strategic goals – what they think they're going to end up with
Strategic plan – how they think we're going to get there
Strategic thinking – real issues aside, how can they make themselves look good?

There are various types of strategies too:

> *Business strategy* – they decide who they are.
> *Corporate strategy* – they decide what the company does and where it does it.
> *Development strategy* – they think they know what to do but will take it slowly in case they're wrong.
> *Dynamic strategy* – they can change their minds at any time…
> *Exit strategy* – for when all goes wrong.
> *High risk strategy*– don't blame them if it goes wrong.
> *Long-term strategy* – there's no hurry: by the time anything is implemented the whole situation will have changed anyway.
> *Low risk strategy* – it won't go wrong because they know the outcome.
> *Service and product strategies* – who's going to do it and what they're going to do it with.
> *Short-term strategy* – get it done before they get fired; a state, for most listed companies, that represents a way of life.

If company leaders are especially worried about what the investors and analysts will think then corporate brochures and reports will be filled with positive images, diagrams and tables, and information on how good their people are.

Take this example: WH Smith is a high street stalwart and one of the most familiar names at airports and railway stations. Throughout the twentieth century and up to the 1980s it went through a period of growth based on sales success; it dominated the markets it traded in, especially books, stationery, and news and magazines. Company results were reported in style with lavish events, TV interviews and general self-congratulatory backslapping allround.

Into the 1990s and competition hit hard: supermarkets started selling magazines and newspapers, then books and music, as those markets deregulated. Independent specialist chains such as Waterstone's nibbled at its credibility and market share. WH Smith couldn't compete on price or range but survived mainly because its stores were historically conveniently positioned on most shopping streets and customers found it easier to go there than to its competitors. Company reports focused on market share and opportunities (especially abroad), expansion into other markets and new channels, as towards the end of the decade opportunities to trade online became available.

In 1996 Smith's suffered a catastrophic year and had to write off large swathes of stock. Described as a 'basket case' by one city analyst, a new management team took over in 1997 and with a 'sexy new broom swept away the old guard'. The company reports reflected this as emphasis was on making investors feel more comfortable; buzzwords like *sales generation*, *shareholder value*, *differentiation*, *customer offer vision*, *synergy* and *innovation* abound.

Shares peaked at over £8 in 1999 as the future looked bright, but the dot-com boom bubble burst and competition hit hard in the noughties as Smith's was relatively slow to take advantage of opportunities that the internet had to offer and failed to fully invest in its high street and travel shops.

Standards slipped, its aged infrastructure creaked and it seemed out of touch (at one stage the management even talked about 'owning the colour blue'). The company became squeezed between the likes of Amazon, the specialists and the supermarkets. Its share was eroded and the management team struggled as they tried to give the company a new image while at the same time dealing with the need to cut costs and restructure and upgrade their systems.

Drastic measures were often taken to make the company look good in the eyes of the financial press. For example, in 2001 Smith's even fell back on that old chestnut – a press announcement about job creation. It's a common PR ploy: take a company in some need of a positive story then make an announcement that it will create, say, 3,000 jobs. It will not only give the impression that it's expanding but that it's a success story in the making.

Attempts at spin in the company communications were usually seen through and the shares dipped accordingly, especially in January 2004 after a very poor Christmas.

Another new management team came in and managed to convince sceptical shareholders and analysts that they were the people to turn it around. This is what the incoming boss Kate Swann had to say…

> We have already taken action to strengthen the senior management team and address the operational short-comings of the business. The priorities are clear – reducing our central costs, addressing stock availability, improving the offer in store, strengthening our controls and processes and addressing our product ranges.

Over the past few years that turnaround has largely been achieved through aggressive cost-cutting, stock reduction and a pretty relentless *drive* to offer value for money. Sales declined on the high street but they have been very successful in airports and stations. The company reports emphasise the success in increasing profits and downplay the fact that this has largely been achieved by cutting costs. Analysts have in general said this is fine, but at some stage the company must improve profits by increasing sales.

Smith's is pretty typical in its attempts to manage fallout and celebrate success in order to keep shareholders happy, using language to emphasise positive messages and play down the negatives. But experienced city-watchers can see through most of this 'blah' and Smith's main public relations problem now seems to be reflected in the sentiment expressed by analyst Paul Smiddy in 2004, who said, 'I am afraid it [WH Smith] is one of those retail names that, if it was not already around, you wonder if anyone would bother inventing it today.'

At the time of writing the main question is how will the current management team manage their PR now that they have been in place a while? Their situation could change rapidly if sales don't come through as needed. No doubt they will increase their profile and succeed in areas such as airports, stations, motorway services and hospitals, but how will they reinvigorate their high street sales? Will they even try?

Words and phrases to watch out for in the context of the way companies want to be perceived are…

Barriers – something getting in the way of success and breaking down those barriers will be a sure way to riches. Usually companies are surprisingly vague about what the barriers are. Often the barrier in question is a person or persons who are on their way out.

Benchmarking – comparing the business to specific or agreed standards; comparing the practices used in other companies in order to improve performance. If you see this word being used then it's a fair bet that a consultant is behind it, as in, 'We'll have to benchmark extensively so that we can get a holistic view of the market in all its guises, then place the company in context. This work should take us, oh, a year.'

Best practice – closely allied to benchmarking, best practice comes into play once the benchmarking has been done. It often hides deep insecurities, relying on copying the success of others to improve business. This means that in reality they probably know little about their own business. Its use is a sign of a company that been used to accepting the mediocre.

Big picture – meaning the wider view. Beleaguered management will exhort observers and investors to 'look at the bigger picture', especially when their actions seem insane, implying that they are somehow aware of facts that everyone else hasn't got.

Comfort zone – an environment or situation in which a person or company feels secure; they feel comfortable as long as there is no drastic change. New managers are encouraged to get out of their comfort zones and take risks, while companies in trouble will talk of leaving their comfort zone. The reality is that many companies spend their time secure in their comfort zone while investors and commentators try their best to move them out of it.

Competitive advantage – an oft-used phrase coined by business guru Michael Porter, who identified two types of competitive advantage: *cost advantage*, where the company delivers the same benefits but at lower cost (see WH Smith), and *differentiation*, where the benefits delivered exceed those of your competitors. The third advantage unmentioned by Porter is the *bullshit advantage*, where the companies that tell the best and most believable lies are the winners.

Continuous improvement – another guru standby; an ongoing commitment to get better both as company and individual. Not surprisingly it's a company report favourite.

Customer value – there are many variations on the 'customer is king' approach to business. Providing something extra for customers is made a company priority, but in all instances the bottom line is always the real king.

Engage – when this appears in company literature it's time to sell your shares.

Focus – another word that signifies that a company is off track.

Framework – a structure around which a business plan is

based; a word lumped together with *template* and *structure*. It signifies the need for control, something to build plans on. Managers able to work in a fluid situation are viewed with suspicion by others, especially by the company yes-men who need a rigid structure to climb up.

Gold-plating – not something you'll see in a company report specifically, but this is the name of the technique of overplaying company value or management ability.

Hit the ground running – a common phrase used by new owners, MDs and leaders.

Innovation or *innovative* – this should mean that the company in question will be launching something new and original. The idea is that, as an investor, you will be turned on by the term. However, although senior managers will often call for innovation in their company, they don't know what true innovation is. And when something innovative actually occurs their instinct is to resist it as it means a change in the status quo, something that they are very wary of in general. Few companies truly innovate, although they will happily steal the innovations of others and represent them as their own if it's in their interests.

Joined-up thinking – when people have separate conversations there are lots of ideas being created, and the process of gathering those ideas together to form a plan is called joined-up thinking. It's usually used when a company is being turned around and the new management is keen to diss the previous leaders.

Journey – this one usually comes out during the presentation of company reports or results. Pass the travel sickness pills.

Lateral thinking, thinking outside of the box, work smarter – in other words, the company has run out of ideas or is desperate. Also watch out for other terms such as *brainstorming, barnstorming, blue sky, stretch the envelope, get granular* or *to go deep diving.* Avoid them all!

Leading edge – companies are fond of calling themselves 'leading edge', as if they are in the vanguard of their field or the foremost in the market. However, type 'leading edge' into Google and 31 million responses appear. For years business gurus have encouraged companies to be one step ahead of their competition, to be future facing, innovative and to lead the market. Obviously, then, some companies are claiming to be leading edge when they clearly aren't, so do we have the real thing, corporate bullshit or just pure self-delusion?

Learnings – usually mentioned when something goes awry and the company in question wants to limit the damage. Sometimes it's *lessons learned, key learnings* or *learning points* – whatever the term you can be sure they're hiding something. Often seen in the literature from sports-related companies, such as football clubs.

Make it happen – a plan is in place, a strategy has been formulated and now we just have to do it!

Making a difference – this is something all new leaders

want to do; whether that difference is good or not is another matter.

Market leading – most company bosses dream of leading their chosen market; some dominant ones actually do, while some claim to actually widen or change their chosen market with their latest products or campaigns. In reality, it's often more to do with economic factors than marketing, and leading the market doesn't necessarily mean the company is profitable.

Market share – mentioning market share in a company is usually a sign of a fallback position. Companies only highlight market share when the rest of their performance isn't worth mentioning.

Paradigm – this is a commonly used weasel-word, mainly because many people are unclear what it means. *Webster's Dictionary* defines this as follows: 'A set of assumptions, concepts, values, and practices that constitutes a way of viewing reality for the community that shares them, especially in an intellectual discipline.' This book, then, is about the paradigm of deceit in common business parlance. If it achieves a change in the behaviour of people and the way they use language in business, then a *paradigm shift* will have taken place.

Passion – you'd be forgiven for thinking that business people are a passionate bunch, but the reality is they are pretending: anyone who tells you that they're passionate about paper clips, widgets, spreadsheets, paperwork or any remotely dull product is boring, lying or mad.

Proactive, not reactive – a common mantra among executives, meaning to anticipate and act with forethought instead of waiting for something to happen before taking action; usually it's a sign that it's all too late. There is one related phrase that companies in trouble often use: 'If we keep doing the same thing, the same thing will happen.' Another related mantra is *work smarter*, although few seem to know what it means in practice.

Targets/KPIs – companies should be obsessed with achieving their targets but whether the right *Key Performance Indicators* are in place – well, that's a different matter. One to watch here is performance-related bonuses.

USP – the *Unique Selling Point* is essential for companies to differentiate themselves from their competitors; it's still widely mentioned as a justifying factor, especially in getting more funding.

Within our gift, in our hands – common among struggling premier league managers, usually it ends up being interpreted as 'only we can get it wrong'.

World class, class leading – meaning outstanding or the best there is. When this appears in company literature it's usually a sign of self-deception. Over-confidence always leads to failure. One signal term common here is *on a roll* or over-the-top praise from the leader for their management team – usually the time when companies start to convince themselves of their genius and, if you're a shareholder, the time to get out.

3

Figures of Speech, or Corrupting English in the Name of Business

'English has borrowed from everywhere and now goes everywhere.'

Mason Cooley

Business English is full of ridiculous sayings, phrases and weasel words and nothing more than old wives' tales disguised as rules. Entertaining though these all may be, they often cause confusion and can leave the user open to ridicule, and they can be used to intimidate or to obscure the truth.

These are the most common types of figures of speech:

Antonym – a word that is the opposite of another, so *hot* is the antonym of *cold*.

Aphorism – an original thought or concept expressed in a short sentence; for example, Ralph Waldo Emerson's, *Nothing great was ever achieved without enthusiasm.*

Axiom – a self-evident truth. One of the famous Zurich Axioms is, *Distrust anyone who claims to know the future, however dimly.*

Cliché – many of the terms listed in this book as 'bad' have lost their original meaning and the intentions meant by their author; in other words, they have become clichéd. Clichés are often formed from metaphors, aphorisms and other sayings that have become hackneyed through over-use; for example, when a new MD takes over a company and announces that they're *going back to basics.*

Euphemism – a phrase used to replace a potentially rude, controversial or harsh term with one likely to cause less offence; for example, *to let one go* instead of *sack.*

Idiom – an apparently nonsensical phrase applied to an act or one that disobeys normal grammatical rules; for example, *kick the bucket* or *laugh your head off.*

Metaphor – a term or phrase applied to something that isn't literal but applied in resemblance; for example, *The sea is my mistress.* An allegory is similar to a metaphor but is extended into a story that is told to imply or give meaning to something.

Mixed metaphors – sentences that combine or link two disparate ideas or elements; for example, *Don't eat with your mouth full* or, *Do you follow where I'm coming from.*

Simile – a figure of speech where two (or more) things are compared; for example, *cunning as a fox.*

Synonym – a word that is an alternative meaning for another or one used as an alternative; for example, *to action something* instead of *to do something.*

Visual metaphors are those that create descriptions using imagery. I once attended a conference in which the speaker likened the company that he'd just bought to a Formula One motor-racing team. He wanted to show how he'd turned the company from a loss-maker into a profitable concern.

He started by saying that when he took over the company was like an Formula One car that had gone 30 laps; low on fuel, with worn tyres and in need of a pit-stop. He even got in a dig at the old management by mentioning that the 'driver needed a rest'. He went on to show he refuelled the car (motivated the team), put on new tyres (better systems), upgraded the steering (new strategy), improved the brakes (better financial controls) and put new rubber on the road (better stock), and, of course, he changed the driver (sacked the management). He overtook competitors and was now on the way to taking the checkered flag.

His speech was enjoyable for many in the audience, but was lost on some listeners who knew nothing of motor-racing. Confused by the metaphor, they missed the message about how he'd taken a tired company and changed it for the better.

Using visual imagery can be a clever way of making a point: it can be used to deflect the attention away from a problem, to impart information in an entertaining way or to reinforce a position. But it is important to be aware of your audience and how they are receiving your message.

My conference speaker friend could have given a more conventional allegory than a racing one, which – while possibly less entertaining – could have ensured that his message was received by all of his audience. Alternatively he could have stuck with the original story and followed it up with another for those who didn't understand his first effort; this also gives the opportunity to reinforce his message.

Let's take a few real examples of companies using this mixture of idiom, stories and buzzwords to explain what they do and to sell themselves and their services. This is from a real company website where we are invited to learn about the tactics they use to 'release aesthetic creativity'…

Tactics include: story-building methodologies to provide a person or group with the skills and flair to translate a situation into a story; common symbols to be a vehicle for a community whereby they can transform the decisions and intentions of a community into objective art forms; decor context to broaden the scope of decor artefacts to include various dimensions, such as time and space; seminal culture exposure to occasion artistic events and art forms through which another culture is dramatized or revealed; and media presentation to expand the frame of reference out of which the content of media flows. An example of this is the development of holography giving a new dimension to man's visual awareness.

This is annoying on two fronts: it sets out to create mystery about a company that certainly isn't there, and then it uses overly complex language that for most people obscures any meaning.

It's intimidating for some to be faced by this as they don't understand it and are afraid to ask questions about it – they don't want to look stupid. The company concerned probably thinks it looks really clever, but its message is lost.

One reason why companies feel the urge to fluff up their sales pitch is because they feel the need to produce something new that hasn't been said before. The pressure to be different, to be fresh and stand out from the crowd means that many companies flesh out otherwise straightforward pitches with gobbledygook. Those experienced in receiving this type of pitch usually interpret this as a case of style over substance and react accordingly.

Companies that use this type of language *can* succeed in bringing fresh ideas to a company that's grown stale, but there is often a culture clash when a suspicious workforce reacts against it.

Selling is a difficult art at the best of times; here we have a company selling promotional space within large stores. Under the heading 'Solutions' we get:

Utilising sophisticated IT systems to back up national relationships allows Company Name to pinpoint avail-ability in a variety of Venues.

Working With You
Utilising Company Name's Campaign Management solutions allows brands & promotional companies to dominate the channel to consumers in UK wide venues. Company Name works closely with clients to deliver quantifiable campaigns & results.

Solutions in a Box
Company Name supplies a one-stop solution that matches client needs & extends beyond simply supplying promotional space to encompass dynamic & inventive Campaign Management solutions.

Customer Care
Company Name recognises that multi-site manage-ment of busy venues requires an extra level of customer care to ensure the smooth running of successful campaigns. With a dedicated approach to account management, Company Name ensures that the expectations of busy clients are met & exceeded.

Not only do you get hit with a large number of action-orientated words, but they contrive to mention their company name six times. They show the company as though it's a person, which is slightly sinister and pretty irritating. The whole website is written in this style, which means it becomes very tiring to use and prospective clients may lose interest.

Working on the 'I have this much space to fill so therefore I must use it' principle, companies often alienate potential customers by being too verbose. In nearly all cases it would be very easy to edit their message down to a few bullet points that everyone can understand. It's all too tempting to add gloss, exaggerate, glorify or use more complex language than necessary in order to come over as particularly literate or more intelligent. Perhaps you'll forgive me for citing one of the most famous figures of speech used in business – *less is more.*

Many people are suspicious of over complicated or flowery language; the question they are most often asking themselves is, 'What are they hiding?'

4

The Liar's Best Friend – the Euphemism

'"Women's fashion" is a euphemism for fashion created by men for women.'

Andrea Dworkin

Using a euphemism is the most common linguistic technique for disguising something bad or an event that could otherwise be awkward.

One of the best examples of euphemisms at work is in those departments that manage people's employment – the Human Resources department or, as they often like to call themselves these days, the People Team. Getting the sack is rarely pleasant but the process is dressed up in any number of ways to soften the blow or make the person doing the sacking feel good about the process and themselves. Some terms are remarkably vague while others are pretty blunt. Here are some examples:

Axed, *bust*, *chop*, *cut*, *fire*, *terminate*, *canning*, *canned*, *ditch* – these indicate a forced removal or at least to go on the grounds of some sort of misconduct. The person being *shown the door* has done something to be ashamed of; the company concerned doesn't want to wash their dirty laundry in public.

Blood bath – a massacre, a period when there are lots of sackings. The theory is that by announcing the sackings all at once, all the publicity happens in one go; it may also hide many other issues that the company involved doesn't want to advertise. Those left after a blood bath are usually described as the *walking wounded.*

Collect your P45 – for those of you not in the UK, the P45 is a personal document that passes between employers; it's given to the employee as they leave.

De-recruit, downsize, re-engineer, restructure, right-size – all terms used to make the fact that a company is sacking lots of people more palatable, and to give the impression that more is being done aside from just sacking.

Dismissed, get the boot, get your marching orders – more militaristic overtones and the impression that there is a lack of honour in the going of the person being sacked.

I want him/her out – the cry of a manager desperate to get rid of someone, usually to the HR team, who then have to facilitate the exit, often by transferring but occasionally by more devious means – 'Go now with a good reference or later with a bad one.'

Lay off, let go – usually to do with redundancy, an attempt to soften the blow by softening the words. It doesn't work. Redundancy is the standard process by which companies reduce their staff. For some, this carries the wrong overtones: they prefer it all to be voluntary or to have it said that they resign.

Euphemisms abound in the recruitment side too. Take these terms (and what they could really mean) that appear regularly in the job adverts…

Achievement orientated – here you take as read that you'll get lots of targets to aim for.

Clarity of vision – in other words, they haven't a clue what to do next so they need someone who can tell them…

Commercial acumen – they need someone who knows what a P&L is.

Communication skills – no one is talking to each other and they need someone to mediate.

Decision maker – they need someone to blame when it all goes wrong.

Development – it's a case of getting you in before you develop enough skills to be classed as a senior manager; it's cheaper.

Dynamic – someone's needed to do the work.

Energetic – 'now you've finished that, the boss's car needs washing.'

Enthusiastic – they need someone who likes their ideas.

Exciting – they need to liven the place up.

Flair – they don't want anyone who they consider boring or dull.

Highly organised – they're in a mess.

Innovative – read as young.

Interpersonal skills – they need someone who can actually talk to other people without embarrassment or being embarrassing.

Leading – leading what?

Lifestyle – no working class people need apply.

Make a difference – they've run out of ideas.

Money motivated – low salary, high bonus and unachievable targets.

Negotiation skills – all their current deals are just rubbish.

Numerate – they need someone who knows how to work Excel.

Opportunities – meaning risks, or at least the chance to clear up someone else's mess.

Portfolio – they want you to do variety of tasks, but haven't thought what they could be, and they think this might make the job sound bigger than it really is.

Presentation skills – they're scared of PowerPoint or presenting.

Proven success – they're hoping it will rub off on them.

Reputation – great, you've done it before.

Stakeholder – if we like you we'll give you some shares, eventually.

Step up to the challenge – because they can't.

Supportive – they need a brown-noser to tell them how great they are.

Team-building skills – they can't manage their people.

Look at any high quality daily paper and you'll see these terms littering the job adverts; rarely are they bullshit free and the reality often isn't anywhere near the claims.

Euphemisms are common throughout the corporate world. Here's a few more to watch out for and avoid:

Bumpy ride – a stormy period for a company; for example, when they are being taken over aggressively or are victims of a fluctuating market. Leaders will point to market forces or global phenomena and mention this term several times as a way to cover up their shortcomings.

Dancing round the handbags – to prevaricate, put off making a decision – 'Stop dancing round your hand-bags and get on with it…' Borrowed from the dance floor habit of piling up the handbags in the centre of the group.

Dog's bollocks – from the premise that a dog is so fond of licking its testicles, it follows that there must be something pretty good about them. So this phrase actually means something outstanding. It's a favourite saying of senior managers who want to appear as 'one of the lads'; the ones to avoid.

[Going] Deep diving – meaning the process of detailed analysis combined with problem solving. Colleagues will probably think you're extra clever for using this one. Some people don't *deep dive*, they *get granular.*

Drinking at the last chance saloon – someone described as doing this is always on the verge of being sacked or, when applied more broadly, this can mean a company going bust.

Fence mending – repairing relationships. For some reason, this is usually applied to political relationships, but most managers spend their time *mending fences*, *building bridges* and *knocking down barriers.*

Food chain – the competitive hierarchy derived from the biological system where the weak are preyed upon by the strong. *Survival of the fittest* is also often heard in this context. Getting to the top of the corporate food chain is the goal of most ambitious company bullshitters, or at the very least the top in their little pond.

Gold-plating – a euphemism from the world of company takeovers, where the company being bought deliberately overplays its value to get a better share price.

Grasp the nettle – take the opportunity without fear, even though it may hurt a bit. The reality is that it will hurt a lot. This is best said in a Welsh accent.

Magic bullet – In desperate times, when their forecasting has failed and they are far from hitting their budget, finance directors are known to prowl their business looking for a solution that will save them and their company: the *magic bullet*. The poor fools will also be looking for *pots of gold* too...

Open heart surgery – another physical impossibility but a company needing this is in real trouble; of course, new management will always want others to believe it's worse than it is so that when recovery happens it looks all the better.

Pear-shaped – meaning gone wrong or going wrong. There doesn't seem to be an obvious origin for this term except that maybe something that was meant to be circular went pear shaped.

Reinventing – a company makeover, to change back but with a new form. The saying 'we don't need to reinvent the wheel' is a common cry among people who resist change or don't want to spend money on change. This word appears in many guises; for example, companies will be advised by gurus to *reinvent themselves* after something's gone wrong in order to present a new image.

5

Metaphors, Many and Mixed

'The metaphor of the king as the shepherd
of his people goes back to ancient Egypt.
Perhaps the use of this particular
convention is due to the fact that, being
stupid, affectionate, gregarious, and easily
stampeded; the societies formed by sheep
are most like human ones.'

Northrop Frye

It's true that without metaphors business would be less entertaining. It's possible that without them creativity would be stifled and many successful business concepts that we are familiar with today just wouldn't be in common usage.

However, as we've seen with euphemisms, metaphors are widely misused and here are just a few examples:

All singing, all dancing, bells and whistles – it does everything. It (usually a deal or product) comes with everything included and more. Whoever says this is usually keeping something back; be suspicious.

Back on the coal face – the 'coal face' is usually applied to the point where customers meet the company – a shop, for example. Someone who works at head office is often described as lacking experience at the 'coal face'. Managers will use this term as a badge to improve their credibility and as a euphemism for hard graft or a *back to basics* approach.

Ball juggling – the act of coping with several tasks at once, akin to a juggler juggling several *balls in the air*. Some will say that management is all about keeping as many balls in the air as possible; it's also about keeping *spinning plates spinning* and any other multi-tasking imagery you care to name. It's used by those who just want to appear busy, but beware managers who talk constantly about how big their team is and how much their turnover is, just to impress – with more than six direct reports, they are either exceptional or their boss is setting them up to fail.

Between a rock and a hard place – meaning to be caught between two unpalatable solutions. A very common occurrence in business, but when a staff member is asked to do something that they know is fundamentally wrong usually they haven't the courage to tell the boss that. They know that if they do as asked and it goes wrong (and they know it will), they'll get the blame, but they're helpless to prevent it.

Building on sand – not very stable. It's often the case that a plan or budget is agreed or built without any basis of fact or substance to the figures, and it may shift considerably from the reality. Usually once everyone knows the budget is not likely to be hit then there are lots of people *drawing a line in the sand.*

Checking the pulse, finger on the pulse – how the business is progressing or the state of play. All businesses can be likened to a living organism, so this is a logical term; unfortunately most company managers have no heart…

Cycling with no saddle – very uncomfortable and often very apposite.

Don't rock the boat, don't make waves – in other words, don't make trouble. This is usually said to a difficult member of a team by their manager in an effort to keep the team working together. Probably a good thing if all you want is to get yourself to middle management and stay there. Listen out for esoteric variations such as *easy tiger* and *you can't boil an ocean.*

Emperor's new clothes – from the Hans Christian Andersen fairytale, in this context it comes in to play when someone convinces themselves that the value of a valueless object is very high. Also applies when a leader follows a hopeless path with his team backing him even though they all know it will end in failure. It's pretty common throughout the corporate world, only in business you don't have the luxury of a small child capable of pointing out the obvious...

Empire building – a term used to describe people who expand their teams and take on bigger areas of responsibility in an attempt to appear indispensable. It's also a good ploy for getting a pay rise as the bigger the team, the more you should earn. *Featherbedding* is an old term from the days when unions had such power they could pressure companies to employ more people than they actually needed to perform a specific task. Less overt is *nest guarding*, which involves keeping information in an attempt to maintain a position of power or to justify a role.

Final piece of the jigsaw – the last piece in place, part of a bigger plan. If you are described as the last piece of the jigsaw, watch out; most companies work on a last in, first out principle.

Level playing field – meaning everything being equal. It's one of the great excuses: 'It's not a level playing field. I can't include that in my budget; it's just not fair...'

Rearranging the deckchairs on the Titanic – meaning

to pointlessly make changes in the face of an impending disaster. This is particularly apt for the period just before a company goes into a disastrous trading period, when management desperately applies unworkable remedies in the hope something will save them; others will go about their daily tasks as if nothing were happening, or *bury their heads in the sand.*

A rising tide that lifts all boats – meaning we're all in this together and whatever happens it will happen to us all. Usually said by a senior executive when referring to a company-wide issue, the real meaning is that they're in the shit and everyone is going down with them. Often followed up with 'when the tide goes out, all the wrecks are visible' – the boss is looking for someone to blame. Some sources indicate that JFK used this term to the effect that everyone benefits.

Wake up and smell the coffee – an exhortation to become aware of something big that's happening. Usually used when a manager wants to rouse their team from some form of lethargy; nowadays the team will just *take the piss*.

Mixed metaphors are sentences that combine or link two disparate ideas or elements, often with unintentional comedic consequences.

The best of both sides of the coin – I've heard this a few times and am still none the wiser.

He cracked it, then blew it... a classic mixed

metaphor; in all probability we've all experienced a variation of this.

The customer is always right – a worthy ambition but in reality an impossibility, it's debatable whether this is really a mixed metaphor in the true sense (maybe an idiom or a dead metaphor), but the truth is that it should be *the customer is always right, providing it doesn't cost too much money.*

I don't know whether I'm coming or going... – obvious sexual connotations here.

In two minds – uncertain (about what to do next); the usual state of most managers.

Iron out the bugs – a common one meaning to clear out any errors.

It defeats the whole object – probably a dead metaphor now: one that has been so over-used that it has become accepted.

Paint a tapestry – part of a sales patter I and some colleagues once received. Apart from the obvious inability to physically be able to paint the said tapestry, the salesman worsened his pitch by comparing his company to a badly performing premier league team which he was under the illusion was doing well.

Shortsighted decision – along with *20-20 hindsight* and most other sight related metaphors, this is just annoying.

Squaring the circle – trying to do the impossible. Sometimes people use *circling the square* – either way, it's pretty confusing.

Talk until blue in the face – an attempt to persuade someone of something for a long time, with no result.

Up their own arse – a physical impossibility for nearly everyone, but possibly an apt description for a pretentious and self-important fool.

In truth I'm not sure using any metaphor in business language is really that bad a thing; it's okay, just as long as everyone knows what is being meant by them, which often isn't the case... For example, take the phrase *It's an outstanding product; it bombed*. To some, this means that the product in question sold exceptionally well, so the phrase is not a mixed metaphor. To others the word *bombed* means the opposite of good, which then makes the phrase a mixed metaphor and therefore confusing – the moral of the story is be aware of your audience and avoid confusing metaphors.

6

The Idiocy of the Idiom

'The great enemy of clear language is insincerity. When there is a gap between one's real and one's declared aims, one turns as it were instinctively to long words and exhausted idioms, like a cuttlefish spurting out ink.'

George Orwell

An idiom is a term that often applies to many different types of phrase; here, I'm confining it to the nonsensical terms that are applied to a business practice or act of lunacy.

Here are a few of the more common examples:

Bang for the buck – determining which idea, task, project or deal gives the best return on our time or investments is what most of us do throughout our daily lives. Those who want to look good while going about it ask which options give 'the biggest bang for our buck'… and they're usually leaning back in the wobbly office chair with their hands behind their head, blessed with confidence that they actually look good while saying it.

Blue sky thinking – one of the best known and most ridiculed business idioms, this is an attempt to tackle an issue or come up with a new strategy or approach by thinking differently, without boundaries and constraints. It is associated with many of the true business bullshit classics such as *brainstorm*, *thought shower*, *thinking outside the box*, and, of course, *stretching the envelope*. My favourite has be the *thought-wok* where ideas are stir-fried…

Chinese walls – a term that originated from the 1929 stock market crash where an imagined wall was put up; it's when information trading is prohibited because of mutual interest, say between two companies owned by an umbrella company. You can almost guarantee it's a complete sham, especially when stakes are high.

Cooking with gas – underway, making rapid progress. This saying makes no sense.

Ducks in a row – to present a united front, be well organised and equally informed in advance of an event; its use signifies a certain level of paranoia. Another famous phrase, *singing from the same hymn sheet*, means much the same thing.

Eating your own dog food – the fantasy process of actually using something that you have created and the realisation that it's rubbish.

Left hand not knowing what the right hand is doing – more a euphemism for a lack of communication where people acting in a certain way assume that their colleagues are doing the same. It's a classic, and incidentally a very common occurrence in the real sense in businesses everywhere.

Low-hanging fruit – self-preservation may keep you from laughing when this is used, but if your boss says to you that there is no low-hanging fruit in your department, take it as a compliment as it means that there were no obvious opportunities to make easy or quick sales or cut costs. The term *quick win* is a favourite too; it means much the same thing but is less entertaining. These terms will be used to give the impression that the facts have been thoroughly investigated and no opportunities are available.

Mad as a box of frogs – unpredictable, totally barmy and an excellent term that applies to most offices, teams and work situations that involve many departments in a large business.

Open the kimono – amazingly some people actually use this term. It means to open the books to auditors; to expose something previously covered up.

Pushing (or *stretching*) *the envelope* – the theory is that the envelope in question is a technical term relating to the performance of fighter aircraft, with the envelope being the limits of its technical abilities. In all, a pretty odd way of saying, 'How can we do more?'

Riding the razor blade – close to failure, with disastrous results if it all goes wrong; one of those phrases, like *cocks on the block* or *going tits up*, that brings a wince when you think about it too much.

Rocket science – meaning something incredibly complicated, usually used in the negative – 'It's not rocket science, after all' – when referring to something simple that has been done poorly. Well, except rocket science itself, nothing is rocket science, is it?

Second-hand bullshit – meaning a repetition of other people's lies; not a pleasant thought in practice.

Smoke and mirrors – a trick played by politicians and PR-orientated managers and generally something ephemeral that hides the true, more serious situation.

Stake in the ground – state a specific position.

Someone has to start negotiating from somewhere and someone has to make the first move in any type of negotiation… but where to put the stake!

Tick the boxes – achieve everything, taken from an imaginary checklist. This is the province of the back-side-coverer, the paranoid and the risk averse.

Ticking time bomb – a business disaster waiting to happen; variations include *tiptoeing through the mine-field* and *avoiding the grenades*.

When the going gets tough, the tough get going – the strong always rise to the challenge. A classic management *call to action* to be said when the team is under pressure, usually with a clenched fist punching the invisible foe. Try not to laugh.

Whistling past the graveyard – ignoring a serious or impending problem while knowing it's there all the time. This is a constant theme through company life; many problems never get addressed until it's too late. Bullshit rules.

7

Smile, It's a Simile…

'Simile and Metaphor differ only in
degree of stylistic refinement. The Simile,
in which a comparison is made directly
between two objects, belongs to an earlier
stage of literary expression; it is the
deliberate elaboration of a correspon-
dence, often pursued for its own sake. But
a Metaphor is the swift illumination of
equivalence. Two images, or an idea and
an image, stand equal and opposite; clash
together and respond significantly,
surprising the reader with a sudden light.'

Sir Herbert Read

In this short chapter we look at that term that always seems to bring a smile to the smug user as they come up with a clever association or witty comparison.

The recent rise in the use of the simile has to be down to the work of one man: motoring journalist and pundit Jeremy Clarkson. It's difficult not to review cars using similes, but Clarkson has it *down to an art-form*. Here are a few of his:

'Much more of a hoot to drive than you might imagine. Think of it, if you like, as a librarian with a G-string under the tweed. I do, and it helps.'

'It looks like it might kick your head in... for fun. Especially in black. In a pale colour or silver, it looks like Vinnie Jones in one of Graham Norton's T-shirts.'

'Racing cars which have been converted for road use never really work. It's like making a hard core adult film, and then editing it so that it can be shown in British hotels. You'd just end up with a sort of half hour close up of some bloke's sweaty face.'

His popularity, especially in the UK, means that it feels like all motoring journalists seem to speak like this, as they try to outdo him. This in turn has led to a significant proportion of British management attempting to spice up their everyday language with a smattering of similes. Not good.

As easy as ABC, 123 or falling off a log – it rarely is, except perhaps losing money.

Cookery – business is not like cooking unless you're

71

Jim Leng, the chairman of the steel group Corus, who said this while going on the defensive about the company's merger with Indian conglomerate Tata: 'We didn't cook this deal up. It wasn't microwaved. This was like an Indian curry where you've got to marinate the ingredients for a long time'

Journeys – it's common for managers to describe their companies as if they are going on a journey, particular when they are in a recovery phase. It's when they add unnecessary details to liven up the story that it becomes awkward. Business gurus love journeys too, usually the *journey to excellence* or the *path to reality* or the *trail to…* Eventually you'll get *back on track*. Have you ever noticed how many businesses *fly*, *drive* or *sail*?

Drive that message home or *drive sales* – these are widely used. *Drive* is a word that has some 40 different meanings and uses depending on the context. *Drivers* (and *levers*, *wheels* and *cogs* for that matter), are considered the key elements that 'propel' any business, so in retail they are sales, gross margins, costs and so on. Then you have the *road map*, then *pit stops*, *barriers*, *detours*, *lay-bys* and the odd *breakdown*. If it all goes wrong then *the wheels fall off…*

Flight path, *flight plan* – meaning the route to take or how something such as a project is progressing. People talk about *navigational aids*, *turbulence*, *mid-air refuelling*, *runway lights* and (with the odd crash) *landings*.

Like a missile – comparing a top salesperson to a missile (usually an Exocet) is meant to be complimentary but the reality is that they are thought of as one dimensional and only have the one talent.

Like herding cats – I once managed a team that consisted of some 30 people, all female, made up of senior buyers to administrators. I described the experience as *like herding cats*. Anyone who has attempted to get one cat to do as they want will know immediately that I meant: that the team was difficult for me (the only male) to manage. Oh how witty I was...

Not comparing apples with apples, comparing apples with pears – a phrase used by the company excusemakers who are looking to defend their decisions by comparing figures that aren't really comparable.

Weddings – how many times have you heard businesses likened to marriages? When someone attempts a hostile takeover it's a *shotgun marriage*, and it's rarely a *marriage made in heaven.*

Most similes used in business can be described with the words of Mr Clarkson: 'If this simile was a form of cheese... it would be Camembert!'

Like all the different types of phrase in this book the simile has its place; often a concept or problem can be highlighted by the use of a clever simile. They are over-used and as we all know *familiarity breeds contempt.*

8

Aphorisms and Axioms

'An aphorism never coincides with the
truth: it is either a half-truth or
one-and-a-half truths.'

Karl Kraus

'It is an axiom, enforced by all the
experience of the ages that they who rule
industrially will rule politically.'

Aneurin Bevan

Aphorisms and axioms are related and seemingly rarely used these days, which is a shame because most contain some relevant wisdom and can save time and bullshit.

To remind you, an aphorism is an original thought or concept expressed in a short sentence; it's about aptness. So we have the following:

'It is not the employer who pays wages – he only handles the money. It is the product that pays wages.' – Benjamin Franklin

'If you don't want to work you have to work to earn enough money so that you won't have to work.' – Ogden Nash

'Lots of folks confuse bad management with destiny.' – Kim Hubbard

'You can't negotiate unless you know the market.' – Harvey Mackay

'You should invest in a business that even a fool can run, because someday a fool will.' – Warren Buffet

'"This Time it's Different" are among the most costly four words in market history.' – John Templeton

An axiom is widely used in scientific fields, especially mathematics; it is a self-evident truth or rule and can be used in business, but it's axiomatic that they are often overlooked and get confused with the hated term, *best practice*.

Popular management books are full of axioms, although

they may come under the guise of business rules. Here are some examples:

'When envoys are sent with compliments in their mouths, it is a sign that the enemy wishes for a truce.' – Sun Tzu, *The Art of War* (adopted business guide)

'Stay close to the customer.' – Tom Peters and Richard Waterman from *In Search of Excellence*

'Without an action plan, the executive becomes a prisoner of events.' – Peter Drucker

Other examples:

'They who rule industrially will rule politically.' – Aneurin Bevan

'There is one rule for the industrialist and that is: make the best quality of goods possible at the lowest cost possible, paying the highest wages possible.' – Henry Ford

'There is no such thing as a free lunch.' – unknown

A false axiom is one that appears true but is patently not so; for example, 'All men are born free and equal.'

I could fill a whole book with these, but what is responsible for aphorism and axioms going out of fashion? Could it be that there is a general lowering in the standards of thought behind communication (known as *dumbing-down*)? Maybe it's because when they are used our natural cynicism takes over…

9

Acronyms

'Tracy Barlow! I mean, even her initials
are a killer disease!'

Eileen Grimshaw, *Coronation Street*

Acronyms hold a special place in the bad language stakes. They are undoubtedly annoying, but they also have their uses. Most businesses and industries have their own shorthand and it's a good opportunity for a certain type of corporate ladder climber to impress with their knowledge. A sad sight, these are the sort who walk around with a load of keys attached to their belts alongside the mobile phone holder, in an attempt to make themselves look more important than they really are.

Here are some really annoying acronyms (gleaned from years of going on courses and listening to consultants) that just get on my nerves:

AAA – Alive, Alert, Aggressive.

ACORN – A Classification of Residential Neighbourhoods, invented by CACI Ltd as a way of measuring and classifying consumers. Bandied about by marketing bullshitters in order to give the appearance of expertise.

AFLO – Another Fucking Learning Opportunity; well, 'We must learn by our mistakes…'

AFTO – Ask for the Order, a salesperson's equivalent to a knot in a handkerchief.

AKA – Also Known as.

AKUTA – A Kick up the Arse.

APE – Attentive, Peripheral, Empathic. Apparently, this is about listening. Salespeople must be able to actually listen to their customers needs rather than just go on about their products.

81

ASTRO – Always Stating the Really Obvious.

ATNA – All Talk, No Action.

B2B – Business to Business. Used by would-be internet entrepreneurs in order to give the appearance of someone who knows about business.

BOGOFF – Buy One Get One for Free. Particularly patronising and usually a sign that either the retailer or supplier is desperate.

BOHICA – Bend Over, Here It Comes Again.

CADET – Can't Add, Doesn't Even Try.

DINKY – Double Income, No Kids Yet. Traditionally the richest group of consumers to be sucked up to.

DNA – building block, make up. The customer's DNA has nothing to do with their biological make up, nor has a company's DNA, or a product's for that matter – it all just makes you want to slap whoever uses this term (usually a consultant).

DRIB – Don't Read If Busy.

EBITDA – Earnings Before Interest, Taxes, Depreciation and Amortisation.

Something everyone who owns a company should know but doesn't.

EDLP – Every Day Low Pricing. A technique pioneered by supermarkets where they price products in such a way that it looks like they have squeezed every last penny on costs, in order to give the customer a better deal. So items normally priced at £4.99 will be priced at something like £4.83. You can bet your life that some poor farmer in the Third World is paying for the 17 pence difference and not the supermarket in question.

FIFO – First In First Out.

FMCG – Fast Moving Consumer Goods.

FOBIO – Frequently Outwitted by Inanimate Objects. Okay, so maybe this is a bit personally apposite but isn't it funny how the most calm, patient people can turn into psychopaths when it comes to adjusting the office chair…

FOC – Free of Charge. In the world of business, nothing is FOC.

FORCE – Focus on Reducing Costs Everywhere. The mantra of certain accountants and new MDs and finance directors who want to make a mark; they do this not by creating revenue but by cutting costs in the hope that everyone will work harder to make up the difference. Invariably in time this ruins the company.

FUCT – Failed Under Continuous Testing.

FUD – Fear, Uncertainty and Doubt. Some managers like to breed an atmosphere of FUD as a way to manage people; eventually their team will turn to glorious revenge.

GLAM – Greying, Leisured, Affluent, Married and the

fastest growing consumer group in the western world.

IDEAL – Identify, Define, Explore, Action, Look back.

IMHO – In My Humble Opinion. Well, it's not humble at all, is it? To be lumped in with the classic *with respect*.

IPATTAP – Interrupt, Patronise, Argue, Threaten, Terminate, Apply Penalties. This is presumably what passes for customer service in the banking industry.

JFDI – Just Fucking Do It.

KAS – Knowledge, Attitude, Skills.

KISS – Keep It Simple, Stupid. One of the most patronising acronyms, so therefore one of the most used.

KPI – Key Performance Indicator. These are the lifeblood of any financial manager; they enable them to monitor how the business is performing to a set of predetermined criteria. Many businesses, when they discover the joys of using KPIs, go mad, overusing them and putting their staff under strain. The trick is to make sure KPIs are attainable and will never be threatened; if that looks likely, someone else will get the blame.

KVI – Known Value Item. This is a line in a supermarket that everyone knows the value of, such as bread, milk and baked beans. Most retailers kid themselves about what a KVI is; most suppliers dream of getting a KVI, especially if they are the only ones who supply it.

LANO – Lights Are Not On.

LAST – Listen, Advise, Solve, Thank.

MBO – Management by Objectives.

MBWA – Management by Walking About (or Wandering Around). A typical management technique or lack of technique, depending on your perspective.

MILE – Maximum Impact, Little Effort. The company bullshitter's motto.

MMM – Measurable, Manageable, Motivational.

NB – No Bullshit. This equates to no entertainment.

PANIC – Pressured and Not in Control.

PDQ – Pretty Damn Quick.

PEBCAK – Problem Exists Between Chair and Keyboard.

PICNIC – Problem in Chair Not in Computer.

POS – Pile of Shite. To some this means Point of Sale.

PPPP (The Four Ps) – Product, Price, Promotion, Place. One of the retail basics, although estate agents seem to have adopted it as part of their patter.

ROI – Return on Investment. As sinister a term as you can get, as this generally comes with lots of implications.

RTFM – Read the Frigging Manual.

SISO – Shit In, Shit Out (also known as GIGO: Garbage In, Garbage Out) – if you input poor data, you get poor results.

SMART – Specific, Measurable, Agreed, Realistic, Time-bound. An old favourite used to brainwash young managers everywhere.

SNAFU – Situation Normal; All Fucked Up.

SWOT – Strengths, Weaknesses, Opportunities, Threats. Beloved by consultants everywhere.

TEAM – Together Everyone Achieves More. When this is said, the speaker usually has their fingers crossed behind their back and is probably thinking 'because then I don't get the blame…'.

TINA – There Is No Alternative.

TQM – Total Quality Management. A blast from the past – management guru jargon from the 1980s; maybe it's time to bring it back?!

USP – Unique Selling Point (or Proposition). I know we all need one…

WOMBAT – Waste of Money, Brains and Time.

WYGIWYD – What You Get Is What You Deserve.

WYSIWYG – What You See Is What You Get.

10
Brands and Brandroids

'A brand for a company is like a
reputation for a person. You earn
reputation by trying to do hard things
well.'

Jeff Bezos

Branding is integral to the style, personality and language that is used in a particular company; its values are reflected in the culture and the people who work there.

Good branding can make a company, while misuse of the brand can destroy it, the best example being Gerald Ratner's colossal faux-pas when he described the products sold in his eponymous chain as 'crap'. The brand is often well used by company leaders as an effective way to give their employees a sense of focus and belonging. As for Ratner, his business suffered accordingly after his speech. So it seems that when it comes to building a brand, you need at least a little bullshit to survive, but it doesn't pay to be too honest.

Branding has its own set of clichés. For example, a *brandroid* is someone who has bought the company line completely, and who then automatically spouts company slogans and lives their life according to the values of the company – usually a sad individual who should know better, and in their heart of hearts they probably do. I've known colleagues to change personality according to the company they work for; it's that effective. Brandroids in turn are responsible for what's become *brandalism*, which is the name for the process of putting the brand on every type of product or clothing (brandwear); just visit a top football club's online shop and you'll get the picture. *Brandwidth* has become the term associated with the level of recognition awarded to a product within a market. And with *brand extension*, companies use their logos on products unrelated to their original use; for example, the heavy machinery manufacturer Caterpillar using their logo on fashion items.

Perhaps the most pernicious use of *brandalism* in recent years is the use of the iconic Playboy logo. For those of you who don't know it, Playboy is a beautifully shot porn magazine (with celebrity and lifestyle articles) established by Hugh Hefner in the 1950s. The Playboy logo is a cute bunny rabbit head, sporting a bowtie, like the famous bunny-girls who featured heavily in the magazine and at Hefner's Playboy Mansion in the 1960s and '70s. Over the past few years Playboy has become more mainstream, aiming itself at a younger audience; for example, the mansion is featured on MTV and there's a blog on Bebo.

In 2005 the iconic bunny logo appeared in blistering pink, black and purple on a range of stationery. Stationers displayed it next to similar ranges from Disney or in aisle-end displays. WH Smith said:

> Playboy is probably one of the most popular ranges we've ever sold. It outsells all the other big brands in stationery, by a staggering amount. We offer customers choice. We're not here to act as a moral censor. We believe it is a fashion range. There's no inappropriate imagery. It's just the bunny. It's a bit of fun, popular and fashionable.

Protests continued but most retailers stuck to a similar line to Smith's, but in May 2008 a vicar, Tim Jones, tore down the displays in a stationery store in protest, saying it was 'wicked' to groom children for their commercial exploitation by the sex industry and at the time of writing stockists are *reviewing their display policies*.

Meanwhile, Playboy says 'We will be *reviewing this situa-*

tion immediately. We clearly did not authorise, nor approve, the placement of our products next to well-known children's characters.' In the words of Tim Jones, 'Well, they would say that, wouldn't they.'

Looking at the products it is difficult to believe in Playboy's statement that goods bearing its famous bunny logo were aimed primarily at 18- to 34-year-olds. However, Hugh Hefner's daughter Christie, who now runs the company, said:

> We all understand that young people, both young women and young men, aspire to grow up, and I am sure that there are young women who would love to wear Playboy merchandise. Whether they should or not is up to their parents to decide, in much the same the way parents have to decide whether someone who is a minor is ready and mature enough to see an R-rated movie.

So both Playboy and the retailers who stock the range take the same stance and that is that they merely put the range out into the market, aiming it at adults, and it's not their fault that the design appeals to young children (who don't understand the implications of the brand).

At best, it's pretty ignorant, at worst very cynical; some would say that it's an extremely clever bit of *brand building*. Whatever your stance, it is a very good example of how brands have a language all of their own that can be just as adaptable as English.

11

Bad Behaviour

'I don't want any yes-men around me. I
want everybody to tell me the truth even
if it costs them their jobs.'

Samuel Goldwyn

In the last chapter we looked at branding and as that is applied to companies, it applies with people too, especially in large companies where workers and colleagues are encouraged to behave in a certain way.

Watch an episode of *The Apprentice* and you'll see the candidates creating images for themselves (with the help of the programme makers), adapting as the series progresses as they evaluate what works and what Sir Alan or Mr Trump doesn't like. Whether it's *giving 100 per cent* or sitting back to watch the others make mistakes, it's all about the image. Building that image is commonly known as *bigging it up* or to some, *giving it large*, *making a play* and so on.

So bad language isn't just about words; it's about how we act at work too. Here are some examples of the typical behaviour that you'll find in virtually every office.

> *Acting important* – a real skill, this involves wearing culturally correct clothes, knowing what to say in meetings without actually committing to anything, using the right body language to suggest power and having an attitude that goes with looking completely confident. It involves walking with a purpose, talking slightly loudly and acting in a seemingly very earnest way.

> *Asking a question while knowing the answer* – this is usually done during a meeting of peers, to increase profile. Sometimes when this is very cleverly done, the question will be one that enables the boss to shine, allowing the questioner to bask in the reflected glory

and to be thought of by the boss in a more positive light.

Being seen around the office – it may seem obvious, but this is an important pre-requisite for anyone who wants to get on: being seen is a must for any attention seeker and go-getter. This may involve turning up early when they know it will be noticed or working late when they know the boss is there. Even when not in the office, the best fakes will leave a familiar jacket or bag strategically placed so that it gives the impression they're around somewhere.

Bumping into the boss – it's important to know the boss's schedule; 'bumping' into them in the corridor, lift, loo or by the coffee machine is a good way to get attention.

Business dress – the best company ladder climbers are not necessarily the smartest in the office; they are the ones that dress most like the boss. Alignment by fashion.

'Can do' attitude – the successful manager always projects a 'can do' attitude; it's an essential part of being successful in a large corporation, a little like *acting important* but with the sleeves rolled up. These people attack every job they are given with verve (110 per cent) in the hope that they'll be seen as top management material.

Claiming credit for the work of others – a classic tactic and one regularly practised by unscrupulous bosses everywhere, claiming credit for others' work requires skill in lying outrageously, bare-faced cheek, plausibility and the ability to keep a straight face as others react when they realise what is going on.

Clapping – a good way to get attention is to clap with hollowed hands; it's louder and sounds more appreciative.

Copying in select important people on memos and e-mails – this kind of attention grabbing is really out of date as it's so obvious, but it still goes on, though is possibly the province of the desperate.

Creating a problem to solve the problem – one of the most difficult self-promotional activities to spot, but one of the most common, typically the corporate fake will call a meeting with their boss and team to discuss a problem that most of them didn't know existed. The team will be dispatched to 'fix the problem' and after a suitable time has elapsed with no success by the team, the protagonist will leap into action to solve the problem, neatly appearing to the boss as a saviour and promotion candidate.

Criticising ex-colleagues – when someone leaves the company, the office fake will arrange it so that their own mistakes can be attributed to the one who left. Those returning to a company they have previously left should be aware.

Employing someone to take the heat then sacking them for failure or taking credit for their success – typically the company weasel will have been given an important task; they will then employ someone to do the work, neatly ensuring that if it goes wrong there's someone who they can legitimately sack in place to take the blame. If the task is a success the fake can still present the work as their own.

Finding out the boss's interests – is the boss a fan of prog rock or hip hop; do they read Dickens or Dan Brown? The company bullshitter will find out and spookily become fans of the same.

Gadgetry – providing the boss is technically aware, being seen with the latest handheld PDA will look good, while the right mobile phone is essential; it must look good and have a ring-tone that isn't tacky but shows some sophistication, so more Arctic Monkeys than Cheeky Girls.

Holding something – no not that! Files, clipboards and laptops are all essential office accessories, and even holding a sheaf of paper makes you look more important, especially if you're reading it intently as you walk. Real aficionados will have files marked 'for MD's eyes only'.

Ignoring what's right – a sure sign of an ambitious grabber and someone who is only looking after number one is when a situation arises in which there is one obvious proper course of action. The fake will ignore it and do what is right for them and their career. It's about looking right, not being right.

Laughing loudly at an unfunny joke made by a director or senior manager – a sad activity, it just encourages them to make more bad jokes.

Putting your name in the footnotes of presentations and spreadsheets – a common, if slightly outmoded trick, as even if the culprits didn't do the work it looks like they did.

Praising the boss – one of the oldest in the book, but it works

Sex – sexy people are the best bullshitters; all their victims think about is how gorgeous they are and all the time they're undermining them, with their short skirts, tight bums and winning smiles... and that's just the men.

Summarising the boss's idea and feeding it back to them – the skilled corporate weasel will listen to what their boss has to say, pull out the salient opinion and replay it back to them using similar words. This gives the impression that they are on the same side as the boss and understand fully what he/she wants. Faking empathy is a great skill; it can appear insincere but when it works it's very effective.

Taking the lead during presentations – 'You're only as good as your last presentation' is a motto often followed by the most successful fakes. Have you ever noticed how the best presenters always get on?

Talking loudly – one for open-plan offices, the technique is to wait for the boss to be around, then be heard talking on the phone using words and phrases like 'the numbers', 'deal', 'contract' or 'customer', bandying these about along with sideways glances to see that the boss is listening.

Walking purposefully – the walk is very important; it is essential to look like an important mission is involved, one that is vital to the future of the company. Ideally you must carry a clipboard or piece of paper, though the real aficionados will be walking round with envelopes marked 'For Chairman's eyes only' or 'Confidential'.

As everyone knows, the skill of *bigging it up* is about how good a liar you are and a lot depends on not being spotted or how you deal with the lie once you've been found out. So how do you spot a liar?

Latest research being undertaken by the University of Texas shows that the stomach reacts differently when the subject is telling a lie. The current method of lie detecting measures stress patterns in the heart and also through levels of sweat, but practised liars can cheat it. Apparently the stomach test (called an electrogastrogram; EGG) is pretty infallible.

However, we can't carry a whole mass of kit around with us; imagine strapping your boss, colleague, customer, supplier or competitor into a lie detector every time you wanted to have a meeting. But now, using the information in this book, you can hopefully spot a bullshitter. So how do you know when they are lying to you without the aid of machinery?

Here are several key pointers gleaned from the work of several experts. Remember that individually they don't point to a liar, but these 'signals' seen in clusters can help in identifying deception:

1. They don't know you well. The better they know you, the less likely they are to lie, as they know that you are likely to be aware of behaviour that is outside their norm. However, they may well decide to risk it and, if they are practised liars, it won't stop them anyway.

2. They fail to make eye contact. You may find the inexperienced liar looking away as they speak. Look for the 'liar' who is looking at the spot between your eyes rather than directly at them. Alternatively the person concerned may just be shy or under stress. It used to be said that people who look down when questioned are likely to be telling lies, but this has been proved unreliable.

3. They keep eye contact for a little too long. This could signal a lie; alternatively they may just fancy you.

4. Their voice changes or fluctuates, or they speak too quickly in a rush to get the sentence out or put over information.

5. They shift position as they speak, become unusually fidgety, or hold their body rigidly.

6. They visibly relax when the topic of conversation is changed.

7. They cover their mouth, or put a finger in it, itch an ear or touch their nose. However briefly, and especially if they haven't done it before, it could signal that a lie is being told. Bill Clinton famously did this when questioned about his relationship with Monica Lewinsky.

8. They pull their collar or scratch their neck. This shows anxiety and it's worth questioning further. A defensive response usually signals a lie.

9. They give overly short or overly complex replies. Are the answers to your questions plausible?

10. There's a disparity between what they are saying and their body language. Watch out for anomalies or unusual answers which may appear when the 'liar' is asked simple questions.

11. They don't answer your questions directly or they change the subject. Alternatively they answer your questions but don't ask any of their own.

12. They use words and phrases that you have been using, giving the impression that they are on your side and answering your questions precisely. Often, they will use the politician's trick of answering your questions with more questions.

13. They may absent-mindedly place objects between themselves and you.

14. They stonewall – don't reply to requests for information, for example. The more aggressive they are, the

more likely they are to be lying or hiding the truth.

15. They have asymmetrical facial expressions. These are often touted as a signal to a lie, as it could mean that the liar is not necessarily feeling what they are supposed to show. Beware the crooked smile. At least one expert in the study of lies recommends that by studying facial expressions we can identify liars; it's a matter of looking for discrepancies between what is being said and the expression being offered. Is that smile genuine? Are those nostrils flaring? Lips tightening?

16. They get overly indignant (or don't react at all) when you accuse them of lying.

These are just hints at what could be happening. Being attuned to these signals requires practice in itself, so watch out for clusters of these behaviours. It could save you a lot of grief if, when you pick up on them, you discover you're being lied to or set up, but unfortunately there is no one signal that can point to a lie.

One problem in identifying liars in any situation is that you can be overloaded with observations that contradict each other; there's too much to take in. Try not to use 'gut feel' to identify the liar: research shows that it generally doesn't work, so it's better to assume you're being lied to, especially during a negotiation or when dealing with a competitor. Think about the situation you find yourself in and place yourself in the other person's shoes. Don't be afraid to ask questions and if in doubt walk away.

It's axiomatic that lying is an essential skill in business and especially in leadership, when it's not necessarily about the lie but how good a liar you are.

12

(Mis)Leading

'The world is formed by unreasonable
men. A reasonable man looks at the world
and sees how he can fit in with it. An
unreasonable man looks at the world and
sees how he can change it to fit in with
him.'

George Bernard Shaw

So how are all these clichés, aphorisms and metaphors used?

All leaders lie; it comes with the role, after all. It's strange that leaders are often not judged on the lies they tell but how good a liar they are (in a recent survey 90 per cent of Americans said they lied regularly).

Poor liars look out of depth and indecisive or maybe too cocky as they put on a brave face. Good liars get the balance just right: they look honest and in control, and they get away with it. A good example of this contrast in styles and technique is best seen in Prime Ministers Tony Blair and Gordon Brown.

The language of leadership is about producing a good sound-bite as much as anything, so with Blair we have…

'I can only go one way. I've not got a reverse gear.'

'Now is not the time for sound-bites. I can feel the hand of history on my shoulder.'

Each evokes an image and an aim. Blair was also capable of changing his style of presentation according to the situation he was in.

Brown, on the other hand, although he has had much less time as PM, is more interested in 'getting on with the job' than self-promotion. This means that although he may be better at the detail of the role than Blair, he's perceived as being a poor leader by his demeanour and reluctance to be exposed. Memorable Brown sound-bites are rare and it's ironic that probably the one quote he's best known for is something that he apparently said to Blair – 'There is nothing that you could say to me now that I could ever believe.'

Business leaders use the same techniques as Blair in their day to day company lives. It's often about building an image within their company, whether it's as a risk-taker, a cost-cutter or a no-nonsense tough guy (or she-wolf).

One of the foremost business guru's Peter Drucker identified four key competencies that make a successful leader:

1. Listening
2. Communicating
3. Not using alibis
4. Realising that the leader is less important than the task in hand

Presumably included in the communicating bit is the ability to manipulate and lie, but it's not clear.

Dwight D Eisenhower said that leadership is the art of getting someone else to do something you want done because he wants to do it. Language, then, plays an important role in persuading the minions to do what they're told without any problems.

Here are a few examples of the words, phrases and behaviors associated with the dark side of corporate leadership:

Align – a useful word, especially in confrontational situations. 'Are we aligned on this?' allows people who don't wholly agree with the proposition in question to save face. In practice, it means that decisions are postponed or hidden and actions taken outside that arena.

Bang the drum – all leaders like publicity, and often in the corporate world this is not about the company, it's about the leader and their image.

Carve out a niche – whatever your position in an organisation it's good advice to become associated with something good, although too many are given the niche by more experienced managers who like to keep out of trouble. 'Take this project,' they will say, 'it will be the making of you.' Not.

Consensus – leaders hate 'consensual bollocks' but often have to go through the pretence of achieving it. A common trick is to arrange a team day with brainstorming sessions in which pre-arranged agendas have been set up, so that the team thinks the ideas are their own, not the leader's.

Converting plans to action – a leadership mantra if ever there was one...

Custodian – in this context, someone who owns or looks after an important aspect of a business; a stakeholder but not necessarily a leader; someone who the person at the top needs in order to build a successful business. Identifying the key custodians or stakeholders is an important part of leadership success.

Eyes and ears – you know you're in trouble when your manager says 'I want you to be my eyes and ears on this one.' Someone is being set up... probably you. In a similar vein, employees will be encouraged to *grasp the nettle*, to take the opportunity without fear, even though it may hurt a bit. It will hurt a lot.

Go the extra mile, sweat harder, 110 per cent – to do more than is expected. How often do you hear this on *The Apprentice* as the candidates vie with each other to impress the boss? In reality, you'll do all the work and the leader will get the credit. You'll also hear words like *hungry*, *lean and mean*, *eager* or *keen* – the word that most leaders hear, though, is *gullible.*

Gravitas – something most effective leaders cultivate, it's about substance, weight, standing, dignity and respect. Done badly, it can look like they're just acting important and have no substance. Alongside this we have *grown up*. It's generally seen as important to appear to take work seriously; being childish or funny is seen as immature and not a good career move no matter how tempting it is. However, Eisenhower also said that 'a sense of humor is part of the art of leadership, of getting along with people, of getting things done'. So what do I know?

Halo effect – an important part of the leadership toolbox, this is the ability to hog the limelight and benefit from the work of others. A good example of this working at a high level would be the success of the British Forces in the Falklands War and the positive association it gave Margaret Thatcher, who won a subsequent election almost entirely based on the halo effect it gave her.

On a more mundane company level, often those good at making presentations get on well in an organisation because of that halo effect, the logic being that if they are good at presentations, therefore they're good at everything else too... until reality bites and everyone realises that they were just good at presentations.

Heads up – meaning a warning or an update as in 'we must give a heads up to the team', so something is going wrong and the leader wants them to get him or her out of the mire they're already in.

Hidden agenda – a key weapon in the art of leadership, having an undisclosed plan, with an ulterior motive, is integral to the human condition and every successful manager.

Holding our nerve – a common term in times of unrest, many a financial manager is currently being urged not to be panicked into taking unnecessary actions. It's difficult to achieve as the natural human reaction to any problem is to try to solve it by taking action... any action.

Influencer – apart from having strong influencing skills themselves, good leaders need people who have the ability to influence others successfully. Leaders love and hate influencers in equal measures; they know they need them but don't trust them.

In the boss's boat/canoe – I was once told that I was in my manager's boat; apparently I was one of the chosen few, and in line for possible promotion. It went downhill for this manager not long after, and by association the same happened to me.

Knowledge, know-how – what kept me in my job was specialist knowledge. All leaders need specialists.

Long haul – usually when entering a period of uncertainty or a crisis many managers say they are in it for the long-haul and that turning their company around needs time, or is akin to turning a supertanker. In truth, they're waiting for the sack and resultant pay-off.

Making money – it may seem axiomatic that a business is there to make money but at least one leader has seen fit to remind their staff of this fact. I know one who even put it and a list of other objectives in their company Christmas card given out to key managers.

Manage expectations – another key aspect of leadership is to keep expectations realistic, to limit surprises. It's no surprise, then, that managing expectations and bullshit go hand in hand.

On the map – many leaders are out to make a name for their company and to get it known for something, anything, even if it's based on someone else's work.

Outcome or results driven – I mentioned this previously and there's no problem in a leader driving their company towards a specific outcome, so long as they don't become an insensitive, single-minded shit in the process. You can spot a range of phrases and exhortations bordering on pleas, often said as part of last minute panic as a deadline looms: *ramp it up*, *ratchet it up*, *pump up the volume*, *pull out all the stops*, *stoke up the boiler...*

Profile, *exposure*, *reputation and renown...* the lifeblood for any ambitious company leader; at a junior level concerned managers and mentors will advise young colleagues to do anything to get noticed, but often this doesn't involve working hard or getting results – making a good presentation to senior managers is usually enough. Some leaders will do almost anything to get attention, from jumping off buildings to giving large amounts to charity. It's about ego, money and power, not about dignity or generosity.

Radar – most experienced company bosses have an acute awareness about their business and threats, both on a company and personal level. For those lower on the hierarchy, getting seen on the boss's radar is their main priority.

Retaliation, *getting it in first*, *the will to win* – killing off the opposition is a preoccupation with many leaders, both in politics and in business. Doing it with style is another thing; done badly and it can sink a business or tarnish it for many years. An example would be Lucas Industries, which is regularly pilloried for the behavior of its management in the inter-war years when they aggressively expanded the company and effectively killed off their competition. Its role-call of acquisitions is impressive...

1924 Brolt Ltd.
1925 EIC Co. Ltd.
1926 C.A. Vandervell Ltd.
1926 Rotax (Motor Accessories) Ltd.
1927 BLIC Ltd.
1929 A. Rist (1927) Ltd.
1929 Powell & Hanmer Ltd.
1930 M.L. Magneto Syndicate Ltd.
1930 North & Sons Ltd.
1937 Globe & Simpson Ltd.
1937 Bosch Ltd.
1939 Express Magneto (Repairs) & Electrical Co. Ltd.

Each one of these was a competitor (or potentially so), bought during a time of financial turmoil and when product development was very expensive. Had the Lucas management not be so good at negotiating these deals, then there is a strong possibility that none of these companies would now exist, including Lucas itself. There is a fascinating overview of Lucas and its takeovers available from the Competition Commission.

Squeaky clean, *Teflon* – keeping an untarnished, almost too clean image can be important to politicians but it's important for business leaders too, especially those in charge of companies with strong ethical policies. Of course, it takes great skill in the art of *arse covering* to be able to deflect blame and stay above the turmoil that is par for the course with many businesses.

Getting our ducks in a row, *getting our act together*, *a policy of no surprises* and *let's explore the options* are phrases to watch out for when dealing with a Teflon Tony.

Tasking – it almost goes without saying that an important ability for any leader is to be able to delegate and give orders. Tasking, though, comes with deliverables, KPIs, targets and goals, which in turn come with the phrase usually said with threatening undertones, 'You promised me you could deliver this...'

Tenacity – all leaders need this characteristic; the more tenacious they are, the more ruthless they tend to be.

You can do it if you believe you can – many managers say this (or a variation) in an attempt to build confidence in a team. Think about Tony Blair saying it to his cabinet; now imagine Gordon Brown doing the same thing...

And finally on leaders, *incentives*, *rewards*, *bonuses*, *pay-offs* and the *enjoying the fruits of success* – if there's one area in business that attracts more controversy than almost any other it's the levels of pay accorded to leaders.

At time of writing, the biggest bonus ever was awarded to Lloyd Blankfein of Goldman Sachs who was awarded $26.8 million in cash and $41.1 million in restricted stock and stock options, while the biggest dividend ever awarded in British business history was the £1.17 billion the Arcadia group paid to Sir Philip Green and his wife.

These are success stories and you could reasonably argue that these people well deserved their money. But what galls people are the big pay-offs and payouts to people who don't deserve it: those leaders who have led their companies into trouble or who get a bonus even if their company has underperformed.

Adam Applegarth, who led the Northern Rock bank into turmoil and eventual nationalisation, said that he accepted responsibility for the bank's troubles when he resigned, insisting that the catastrophic changes in the credit markets were 'unforeseen'. He may be right, but his bank overly depended on one form of lending for income and didn't spread their risks, so was more in danger of going under when the credit crisis hit.

Applegarth received a £760,000 pay-off and a £2.6 million pension. Roger Lawson, chairman of the Northern Rock Shareholders' Association Group, said, 'Had Mr Applegarth taken the company to court then it could have ended up having to pay him even more, so perhaps it has got away with having to pay slightly less than its legal obligation, so I have to be philosophical about it.'

Perhaps contracts will be rewritten from now on so that 'rewards for failure' can be avoided.

13

Style Over Substance

'If at first you don't succeed, failure may
be your style.'

Quentin Crisp

Leadership brings with it a question that most new leaders have to face: what style of leader shall I be? To some this comes naturally; to others it's a real problem as they wrestle with their image and approach.

In business this manifests itself in the form of distinctive management types, each with their own style and vocabulary. Take these examples of management characters – recognise anyone?

Angry – it's common to find a style of manager who seems always to be on the verge of losing their temper; they get things done because their team is afraid that one day they may actually really lose it and the consequences are too gross to face.

Articulate inadequate – looks great, sounds great and knows nothing. It's about looking good a sharp dresser with great presentational skills. Substitutes short understandable words with longer ones that sound intelligent. So 'below standard' becomes 'sub optimal' or 'example' becomes 'exemplar', while 'analyse' becomes 'get granular' and so on.

Attention seeker – a 'look at me' manager who is always the first up for any task that requires volunteers. They take credit for the work of the team and work hard to impress their bosses. Ruthless.

Chameleon – in it for themselves and no one else, they are excellent liars who will change views to whatever they feel is the prevailing one or the one that gives them best advantage. Ruthless and

119

unpopular with those in their charge.

Charmer – works on the principle that flattery works in all situations. This style of manager works using compliments, unctuousness and the general ability to arse-lick or brown-nose. Style over substance.

Churchillian – great in a corporate conflict, naturally defensive, but always right and with very high (often religious) morals. Given to quoting their favourite leader and very good at rousing speeches. (The Churchill family motto is *fiel pero desdichado* – faithful but unfortunate.)

Conflict avoider – hates any sort of argument, doesn't really like people and manages the team by e-mail to avoid contact.

Deal junkie – just likes doing deals; has no leadership skills whatsoever and turns everything into a negotiation. A frequent user of buzzwords, watch out for, *Come on, let's discuss this, we're in a partnership here...* This person will also commonly send out plenty of emails to colleagues and management, boasting of their deals.

Easy going, nice – (I think this might be me!) not too bothered about deadlines; will use terms like *end of play* instead of 'I want it on my desk by 4pm'. A manager to take advantage of and a leader who is never that successful – too well liked by their team and not ruthless enough.

Fad surfer – I reluctantly use this term but it well describes a manager that adopts each trend in management as it appears, a bit of a bullshitter then, who says whatever sounds right at the time.

Family, mum or dad – this manager type sees their team as their children; very protective, slightly embarrassing and a little mad. Terms like *we're in this together* (they actually mean it) and *one team* abound.

Fighter – without the inspirational qualities of our *Churchillian* friend, this manager is argumentative, protective and overly competitive. However, they are loyal and people will say about them 'you'd want him/her by your side in a fight'. Leads from the front and is the first to volunteer, so is often used by cleverer and more subtle colleagues.

Geezer – a largely male and British phenomenon, they want to give the impression that they're streetwise, hard and a bit of a lad... but everyone knows that they're really from the posh end of town. Liberal use of words like *like, duckin' and divin', pukka,* and *innit* will mark them out.

Goal-setter – a financially motivated manager who is obsessed with setting a target for everything; a product of the '90s and New Labour's fetish for tangible results for everything from hospitals to education.

Hard – one of the most common management styles, they're overtly tough and overly competitive. They 'don't take prisoners' or 'suffer fools gladly'; I once

121

met a very tough manager who greeted me with intro-
duction, 'The name's Hogarth, that's hog for pig and
garth for strength.' Like many, I didn't have the nerve
to tell him that garth didn't mean strength.

Impatient – a manager that is always stressed, generally disorganized and inefficient, and often in danger
of missing deadlines – typically they 'need it yester-
day'. A candidate for a heart attack.

Indecisive – similar to the *conflict avoider*, this
manager is unable to make up their mind, with obses-
sive tinkering with plans and ideas. Not a *completer-
finisher.*

Inspirational – a true leader and when you're with
them you feel great; usually has no substance beyond
the obvious, but 'together we can do it, together we're
a great team…' You're forgotten as soon as you leave
the room.

Lazy – couldn't care less what happens; hoping for the
sack and a good pay off. Bored people who live by the
motto, 'I think you're mistaking me for someone who
gives a shit.'

Machiavellian – possibly the most successful management style given today's media savvy and politically
motivated business world – so subtlety, political nous,
cunning, guile and ruthlessness pick out this deceitful
little weasel.

Mentor – a rare sort, usually already successful; one

who is under no threat of pressure, wise and trusted, great for advice – watch out if they are threatened.

Mushroom – a cliché but an effective one, this manager keeps their team in the dark and feeds them shit. Information is power.

Number addict – another common style, they can't do anything without a spreadsheet to hand. They have an inability to interact properly with people; geek like and eccentric. Often described as a slide-rule manager, they offer the analytical and intellectual approach to management.

Pervert – not interested in anything other than seducing members of their team. Not the sort that you would want to meet in a dark alley.

Power mad – the empire builder attempting to gain more authority through the size of their team, working on the basis that the more people in the team, the more power they have…

Processor – a bit like the *number addict* manager, this jobsworth (often associated with IT) manages by the rule book, has no imagination and doesn't take risks.

Psychopath, *sadist* – like the *Machiavellian* manager but less subtle, they love to watch their team suffer, just for fun, but they are so nice with it.

Puppy dog – wants to be liked and will agree to and say anything just to be popular; a useless manager as this style leads to lots of arguments within their team.

Risk averse – another common type, they won't make commitments in case it backfires on them; similar to the *indecisive* manager but won't entertain new ideas at all.

Ruthless – a quiet type who shows no mercy or compassion. It's debatable whether they enjoy being a complete shit, as enjoyment is something that doesn't manifest itself, but they are not likeable and often have no discernable personality.

Savvy – always aware of what's going on, streetwise and a player, ambitious, articulate and doesn't use business buzzwords. One to watch.

Schizoid – says one thing, means another and does something else.

Seagull – another clichéd stereotype but it's apt for the type of manager who metaphorically flies overhead of their team, makes a lot of noise, lands, shits on them and flies off when the going gets tough.

Sensitive soul – related to the *family* manager, one who cares deeply but, like the *conflict avoider*, manages the team by e-mail in case they say something nasty.

Snooper – this person manages by *snoopervison*: personal intrusiveness, prying and spying.

Strategy manager – someone who has the ability to see only the wider view; they are unable to see the details or, as many managers like to imply, they are far too important to get involved with details.

Stressed – always in a panic; everything is a *nightmare* or a *disaster*. They transmit their stress to their team, who run around in a continual state of excitement, not knowing whether they are doing right or wrong.

Tactician – the opposite of the *strategy manager*, their thinking is to the short term only; they have no ability to think ahead because they are *reactive not proactive*.

Thatcher – possibly dated but used to describe a woman who operates like a man in the mould of ex-PM Margaret Thatcher; huge ability, outstanding presentational skills, high work levels and no life outside work, her home is run like an extension of her company. Works on the principle, 'If you want something said, ask a man; if you want something done, ask a woman.'

The 404 – another apt term from the internet error message, this manager is mistake prone and basically dumb.

Troubleshooter – a manager so busy solving other people's problems they don't do any actual managing of their own team.

Wannabe – related to the *attention seeker*, this style of manager is completely driven by their ambitions; they are self-interested and sycophantic.

Wimp – completely dominated by their team; unable to cope with leading.

Workaholic – does everyone's work for them; doesn't trust anyone enough to actually delegate.

These characteristics and styles can manifest themselves in one person, but one usually dominates. The dominant style will come with its own body language and distinctive jargon and management patois. A good manager will avoid being too typecast unless it's to their advantage. The trick is to know when to stop.

14

Business Isn't War or Sport…

'Kill with cream.'

Anonymous

'A synonym is a word you use when you
can't spell the word you first thought of.'

Burt Bacharach

One of the more irritating traits of business language is the temptation to liken dealings to sporting events or war. It may make the generally dull machinations of business and corporate life more entertaining, but sporting metaphors are generally hackneyed and those relating to battle are usually insensitive, thoughtless and often insulting.

Many managers borrow their favourite sayings from sports, although the sport itself offers up many clichés too – just watch any football match, American or the one the rest of the world play.

Each sport tends to have its own specific language, some of which has found its way into our everyday lives, often without users being aware of the origins...

Ambassador (for the game) – meaning a representative with an air of authority, it's usually applied to a player with some pedigree and a fair degree of gravitas. Companies like to develop people who can play an ambassadorial role, and usually they end up dealing with trade organisations rather than doing any actual work.

Ball park – meaning in the region of. A vague term originally from baseball, but one that most companies work to even if they like to think they are being accurate in their predictions.

Big match temperament – meaning the ability to shine when under pressure or in the spotlight. This is something generally sought after in business.

Bung – a bribe, a discrete reward, now synonymous particularly with football transfers. Bung is also pretty common in the corporate world; it's just better disguised.

Bystander, in the audience, in the crowd – stand by and watch the action. The question usually asked of someone undecided is, 'Are you in the stands watching the game or are you on the pitch as a player?' This is usually followed by, 'It's make your mind up time,' or the more sinister, 'You're either with us or against us.'

Class, class act – stylish, elegant, polished, achievement with aplomb. Management always want class acts in their teams, whether it's a corporation or a sport; it's their interpretation of what 'class' means that is generally the problem.

Counter punch – from boxing; an attack, straight after your opponent has attacked. A *sucker punch* is one you (or they) just didn't see. A good example is the aptly named multi-billionaire investor Joe Lewis who, before the 2008 credit crisis, invested heavily in the bank Bear Stearns, buying up some 10 per cent of the company; in January 07 shares were valued at $170 each, but the bank folded and at the time of writing was being sold to a rival valued at $2 per share. His estimated loss could be as much as $1 billion.

Cover all bases – from baseball; to take everything into account. The province of the conscientious company bullshitter; they won't miss a trick.

Curve ball – from baseball; a tricky and unexpected problem – plenty of these in business. An English, cricketing equivalent may be *bowled a bouncer.*

Done fantastic – from football; performed well. English footballers and managers always leave off the 'ly' in any word that needs it and insert 'done' for 'did', for example, the *boy done fantastic*. Some managers talk in this way in an effort to get some *street-cred*, but somehow it wouldn't sound quite as good if it came out as 'the boy performed fantastically'.

Dream team – the best combination of team members. Times are good, profits are high, there are no personnel issues and everyone in the team is performing very well, therefore it follows it's a great team, a dream team. This is the time to start making changes before it all goes wrong.

Early doors – from football; early in the game. Its origins are to do with the early opening of the doors in pubs. It's another one of those phrases that the more earnest managers use to make them sound like they're really one of the lads.

Even keel – from yachting; keeping the business steady and trouble free. At some stage in their career, every manager discovers that sailing, not golf, is the thing to get into if you want promotion.

Final score – the result. Imagine the MD, having set the over-ambitious budgets and targets, turning to the

131

harassed finance team and saying, 'So what's the final score?' Of course, they know the figures are rubbish, but self-preservation will win over and they will give a favourable answer in the hope they can find something extra to fill the gap during the year ahead.

Fire, full on, passion, pace, pride, total commitment – passion, urgency, will to win, aggression. Many play their sport with fire in the belly. A few managers use it as a management technique and when they do most people don't take them seriously.

From left field – another from baseball; something outside the norm, unexpected. Not a popular event with most managers, who like to be in control.

Game of two halves – from football; this term is a post-match review classic. A good example is the 2005 European Cup Final where Liverpool went three goals behind after an awful first half performance; in the second half, they levelled the match, playing like a different team. This term is regularly nabbed by financial managers in presentations to the city and investors, usually in a matey attempt to explain the variable financial performance of their company. Financial journalists usually see straight through it and immediately sense that something is wrong.

Game plan – from American sports; the planned tactics for playing the game. Everyone in business has game plans: one for doing your work and one for dealing with your colleagues.

Goal – from football; the target. Goals are for ambitious managers everywhere, their reason for being at work.

Go for it – do it, with gusto. Managers who 'go for it' see themselves as great leaders; most managers who encourage others with the term are usually great avoiders.

Head held high – proud, with dignity and the way to behave when it all goes wrong.

Heavyweight – from boxing; meaning important or with gravitas... or just overweight.

Hungry – eager, keen, ambitious. The province of the young and those candidates from *The Apprentice* who give 110 per cent.

In with the big boys now – playing with top clubs or players, top companies, experienced and senior executives. The implication is that they are much more important, mainly because of the direct relationship between money and importance, like nothing else matters.

Lightweight – from boxing; unimportant, no gravitas. In the sexist world of the office, male managers often say this about female managers who they feel threatened by.

Move the goal posts – to change the parameters and adjust targets. If it doesn't look like they are going to

133

hit their targets, many managers will often change the rules or the parameters in their favour.

On a sticky wicket – from cricket; a dodgy position – where most managers are for most of the time.

Plain sailing – from sailing; to finish with no complications. Remember that old cliché about the swan looking serene on the surface while paddling furiously under the surface? Same thing.

Played out of our skins, played with their hearts out – play so hard, bits of body fall off or get exposed. Not a pretty sight; another one from *The Apprentice.*

Play hardball – from baseball; play it tough. An impression some managers want to give, often different from the reality; most are sneakier...

Pump iron – from bodybuilding; it's the high associated with heavy weight training. It's used to mean getting ready for a fight or building up the company in some way.

Punch above his/her weight – from boxing; someone who does better than expected or than their abilities would suggest. Scary for the manager who wants control and predictability.

Put some skin in the game – an idiom for making an investment. It sounds faintly disgusting, therefore good bullshit – possibly to do with leather balls. But can you imagine anyone with an English accent saying this?

Sea change – from sailing; a major change in the weather, meaning a big shift in the state of the business climate. Initiating a sea change is a rare event: usually big changes are not forecast; they happen by chance or when actions are delayed until it's too late.

Step up to the plate – from baseball; be counted, take up the challenge. One for the naïve or ambitious.

Take one game at a time – from football; advice not to overstretch but just concentrate on the immediate future and all will be okay.

World class – outstanding; the best there is. Managers who think they have a world-class team are generally deluded, lucky or are due for a fall.

As if sports analogies aren't irritating enough, many companies culturally resort to the language of war as though it will imbue them with armour in some imaginary battle. Here is where the fighting style of management takes over. This relatively unsophisticated and robust language is mainly used by men; women tend to use cleverer imagery, sometimes even likening themselves to characters such as Atlanta the Huntress or Boudicca and, surprisingly often, she-wolves.

War inspires manager's love, taking centre stage when there's a problem to be sorted or a competitor to be taken on, turning a simple marketing plan into a major field of operations with combatants and the enemy, all the while imagining the smell of cordite filling the air. (In reality, it is usually the smell of bullshit.)

There is one aspect to this type of language that is especially distasteful and this is why it should be avoided. The world of business has no resemblance to the world of war. Some battle tactics may be relevant, but using war terminology is disrespectful to those who actually lose their lives and get injured in the real world. Maybe when using it you don't directly relate it to real battles, but I contend that it has a toxic effect on those using it in business.

I once worked at a company where we were told to 'kill the competition' and I'm sure it created an atmosphere where constructive thought was replaced by the need to live up to the new aggressive way of doing business. It is an industry where having good long-term relationships with suppliers was essential for success and much damage was done with the hostile approach we took to obtain better trading terms. Years later its effects are still being felt.

During this time I noticed that small problems became magnified by the language used, as managers likened potential issues to *landmines* or *grenades*. For trivial errors or events, people used terms to describe them like *nightmare* or *disaster*, which in turn led to much stress and handwringing. The tone was both aggressive and defensive and ultimately doomed to failure.

There is one last reason not to use war-related terms at work. In an office context, it just sounds so ridiculous to use war-related language. Ask yourself how credible do I sound when using terms like these…

Battle ground, *war zone* – usually referring to the market in which the company is trading. A war zone is

Helmand Province, not the high street.

Battle royal – probably originally from cockfighting though more associated with ultra-violent Japanese films, it means an unusually fierce fight where the contestants have no choice but to fight.

Bite the bullet – something has to be done and it's painful; from the fact that before anaesthetics, soldiers bit on a bullet to help cope with the pain.

Fall on your sword – a leader will take the blame and lose their job in the process – usually with a nice financial package.

Front line – staff who work in shops are often described by their management as working on the front line, as though it was a *battle zone*, and there was me thinking it was supposed to be a nice place to be.

Going great guns – going exceptionally well. Apparently this stems from a British naval expression from the 1700s when 'blowing great guns' meant a violent gale. A lot of hot air in practice.

Going nuclear – getting out of hand in a big way.

Grenades – unexpected and unforeseen events, usually trivial.

In the trenches – this is a bit like *battle ground* but the implication is that it's a much harder and longer affair.

It's a war out there – it's a hostile environment. This is a good saying for giving impact, but when it's about something like the toy market, well it's just not a war, is it? Nothing like, in fact.

Kamikaze – to do something suicidal, but not literally. An alternative is *self-toast*, which means much the same thing.

Keeping your powder dry – originally referring to gunpowder, now used primarily regarding keeping something back or not reacting to an initial attack.
In practice, everyone keeps something back except the honest, stupid and naïve.

Lead from the front, leading the line – to take the initiative, be the first, show strong leadership quali-ties. To continue the analogy, those in front always take the first bullets and are first to tread on the land-mines...

Light the blue touch paper – start some fireworks.

Live by the sword; die by the sword – if you live your life aggressively, then there's a high probability that it will end in the same way. Colleagues who act in this way always seem amazed when someone stabs them in the back.

Lock and load – get ready for action. Popularised in everything from John Wayne to *Star Trek*, it should actually be load and lock, but that's Hollywood for you. I once heard a manager say this to his team, which promptly burst into laughter, thereby destroying any positive effect he was trying to create.

Loose cannon – someone who is unpredictable. There is nothing more unsettling for senior management than someone equally senior saying something harmful about the company, albeit with the best intentions.

Minefield – something littered with problems. *Tap dancing in a minefield* is a descriptive way of saying 'doing something and avoiding problems along the way'. Usually those problems are minor.

Mines, landmines – problems. Managers will look at their plans and talk about how to access the *low-hanging fruit*, the *long-term aims* and the *short-term gains*, and then ask if there are any likely landmines on the way; sounds good, like they're on the ball. Troublemakers love laying them; their particular *nightmare* is finding them. Look out for the more esoteric *Molotov cocktails.*

Mission critical – vital to the success of the mission. The main thing here is that everything becomes mission critical.

On the charge – on a roll to victory. Many companies like to believe they're charging to a great victory; sadly many are deluded.

Pre-emptive strike – to attack first in anticipation of an attack from the 'enemy'. One for those gung-ho managers that this type of language attracts.

Shock and awe – a terrifying attack, one that over-whelms the defences of an enemy, from the US attack on Iraq. Why would this have a place in business?

Shotgun approach – take many different approaches towards the same goal, or in other words throw enough shit at a wall and hope that some of it will stick.

Wagons in a circle – from the defensive practice of European settlers, under attack from American Indians, of putting their wagons in a circle. Most people under 30 have no clue what this means, never having seen a John Wayne movie, but that won't stop older managers using it along with w*aiting for the cavalry to arrive.*

Walking wounded – those left bloodied but able to move. Likened to those left after a particularly bloody take-over battle; the poor saps who have to pick up the pieces.

15

Weasel Words

'One of our defects as a nation is a
tendency to use what have been called
"weasel words." When a weasel sucks
eggs the meat is sucked out of the egg. If
you use a "weasel word" after another
there is nothing left of the other.'

Theodore Roosevelt

Weasel words are commonly associated with sentences that begin with the following:

People say...
They say...
It's been said that...
It's been mentioned that...
I've heard that...
The evidence suggests...
It's known that...
It's been decided that...

These are vague terms intended to convey a level of authority by the speaker so that they can develop an argument or pursue their own agenda. They are used to manipulate. The trick here is for the speaker to take the moral high-ground so that those listening do not challenge what they're being told.

Statistics and numbers often play a big role in this type of deception. It was Benjamin Disraeli who, while prime minister in Victorian Britain, said, 'There are three kinds of lies: lies, damned lies, and statistics.' But maybe Churchill was more to the point when he said, 'The only statistics you can trust are those you falsified yourself.'

An example of a common government trick is to play with crime statistics to give the impression that they are managing to reduce crime and make the country a better place. In order to present themselves in a better light, the statistics may or may not count the same crimes reported two or more times by different people, and count multiple offenses by the same person as one crime. The crime may have to be a solid case before being reported as such, and the figures may include suicides as a crime, and estimates on what goes unreported.

Similar tricks are played with employment statistics, immigration and taxes. In retail we commonly get:

Low, low prices
Better than half price sale
Up to 50 per cent off

Nowhere will it say how many items are at better than half price or are actually 50 per cent off, but as long as a certain proportion of lines in a sale or promotion are at these prices then legally the retailer is okay; in the UK the legal level is just 10 per cent.

These techniques are often used by managers who want to justify budgets or push through a pet project so statistics are manipulated to back up their claims. Those experienced in this type of weaselling will have spent many years developing a persona that can back this up – authority and gravitas are the keys to success.

Weasel words come into their own when it comes to excuse making or avoiding embarrassment, blame or possible legal action. Examples include:

Allegedly
Blip
I feel your pain
It was a one-off
It won't happen again

Lessons will be learned
Let me reassure you
Long-term sustainable solutions
Mistakes were made
On the road to recovery
Sympathise
Unfortunate chain of events
We understand
We'll look into it
We'll treat it with the utmost seriousness

Using weasel words as a technique to evade tough questions by the use of ambiguity and prevarication is a common ploy used by politicians, high profile businesspeople and civil servants who are being *economical with the truth*.

One of the most famous examples is Michael Howard's consistent avoidance in answering interviewer Jeremy Paxman's question about whether, when home secretary, he threatened to overrule the director of the Prison Services in relation to the suspension of a prison governor. Paxman asked the same question some 14 times, and each time Howard answered indirectly and, while not actually lying, he avoided what was to him an unpleasant truth. It backfired because in his keen attempts to avoid a direct answer we all assumed Howard was lying anyway.

There are great politicians and awful ones. A common factor is the style of language they use, whether it's to inspire, show leadership, encourage, convince, persuade people to follow a certain path or lie to cover their own tracks. Leaf through the speeches made by great leaders

145

and you can begin to truly understand the power and effectiveness of language.

Perhaps the greatest exponent in UK history was Churchill. At times, Britain's position in World War Two looked like a lost cause, but somehow Churchill's use of inspirational language and his dogged determination meant people backed him in their millions. The politics and the language of today seem a long way away from those times, but there are similarities as modern politicians try to emulate the Churchill effect.

Compare Churchill and Margaret Thatcher: which is which?

1. 'I have nothing to offer but blood, toil, tears and sweat.'

2. 'I am extraordinarily patient, provided I get my own way in the end.'

3. 'Europe will never be like America. Europe is a product of history. America is a product of philosophy.'

4. 'You can always count on Americans to do the right thing – after they've tried everything else.'

5. 'In war, you can only be killed once, but in politics, many times.'

6. 'You may have to fight a battle more than once to win it.'

It's difficult to tell them apart, but numbers 1, 4 and 5 are Churchill's.

Modern politicians in this media age seem swamped by sound bites, spin and meaningless jargon. They and most top business people are media trained to the point where they are loathe to say anything original in case some slip backfires on them. The popular BBC show *Question Time* sometimes catches them out, as they are placed under direct scrutiny by the public. There is a marked difference between the qualities of language used in the responses garnered from an 'elder statesman' like Tony Benn (who has less to lose) compared with the latest front or shadow cabinet junior minister.

One of the best places to hear politicians put weasel words into practice is on radio and TV, when being interviewed on a one-to-one basis. The frontrunners for the best interviewers of politicians remain Jeremy Paxman on *Newsnight*, John Snow on *Channel Four News* and John Humphries on Radio 4's *Today Programme*. All three often bring out the best and the worst from politicians.

Ministers have become media savvy, especially since the 1980s when advertising agencies were first hired during election campaigns. It's led to the term *dog-whistle politics*, originating in Australia: the pushing of subliminal messages in speeches and using specific language that would only be picked by targeted sections of the electorate; like a dog whistle, it's only audible to those it's aimed at.

With so many examples it's hard to know where to start, but one of the most obvious would be a politician demonstrating commitment to one cause that offers a beneficial halo effect, enabling other less popular policies to be more palatable. By extolling the virtues of God and patriotism,

George Bush was able to get policies by the electorate that they would be normally be against.

All politicians have a standard set of now classic words and phrases, used particularly when they are interviewed under pressure.

Take these examples...

Bear with me – meaning stick with me because I want to say something I think is important... and I don't want to answer your question.

Categorical denial – a complete rebuttal of the accusation. If someone offers up a categorical denial they're hoping that by being firm about it the problem will go away; sadly for them, it usually doesn't.

Clearly – politicians who, when making a point, attempt to suggest that everything is straightforward and understandable. Be warned when this word is used because the situation will be anything but.

Demonstrated real leadership – shown that they're not as weak as everyone thought. Several people have supported Gordon Brown with this term in an effort to show that he has actual leadership qualities.

Focus on the issues, not personalities – not insulting the opposition but concentrating on policies and what is actually going to get done. Politicians always say they're going to do this but never do; it's always easier to be destructive than constructive and it gets better headlines.

Going forward – surely one of the most overused and hated political clichés; after all, what other direction could they possibly go? In defence of politicians, when they finally admit a mistake and try to correct it, inevitably they get equal criticism for making a *U-turn*.

Grass roots – local, common people. A patronising term to describe what goes on at the level of politics where people do the real work.

If I may say so – politicians rarely ask permission to say anything so why they say this remains a mystery.

Just let me finish – a classic, usually said while being interrupted and when the politician wants to make a point, no matter what anyone else thinks.

Knows what the country needs, do what's right for Britain – said by a politician wanting to show a fundamental knowledge of what is good for the country: by implication strong leadership against a threat from those nasty foreign types.

Laying the foundations – starting something, something by implication big. In reality, politicians rarely start anything: they lay the foundations, prepare the ground and generally imply things are much more important than they really are.

Man of the people – has an understanding of what people are looking for from a leader; a good bloke with working class values and credentials. It's a term rarely applied to women. It's a difficult thing to achieve as it can be perceived as disingenuous or patronising; most politicians are pretending to understand what the people want, usually based on polls, the media and market research. The worst case by far of a politician trying to give this impression was when then Conservative leader William Hague appeared wearing a baseball cap, reminiscing about drinking pints of lager – he was rightly ridiculed. Since then he has remodelled his image as an elder statesman although he's younger than many of his colleagues. Watch out for the related phrase *ordinary, decent, hardworking people*, which is often used by a senior government person or MP to give the electorate the impression that they're on their side. They're not.

Mandate – authority to do something. These days the term is often applied to the size of a government's majority: the bigger the majority, the bigger the mandate. When a government gets into power with a strong mandate, it doesn't mean that that they'll actually do what they said they would do, in order to get that mandate.

'Of course not, John', *'Yes, Jeremy'* etc. etc. – in an attempt to soften the apparent onslaught from the likes of Paxman and Humphries, the politician under scrutiny frequently calls the interviewee by his or her first name. Sometimes it sounds like they are in a pub catching up on old times and have been best mates for years. This is a very subtle technique borrowed from neuro-linguistic programming, and it appears on occasion to work.

Our children's future is at stake – by implication, storing up trouble for future generations. Tugging at the heart strings here; after all, who would want to hurt the poor little kiddies? Often said by opposition parties, but watch out for U-turns once in power. There's also *we have to look to the future*, which in other words means 'wait until we get into power then we can change everything'.

Taken out of context – words lifted from something said or written but given a meaning not meant by the originator. Politicians are always being either misquoted or having words put into their mouths; it's a sure sign of backtracking...

Will of the people – what the electorate wants, or from the politicians' view, what we want the electorate to think they want.

With respect – another classic, meaning 'I'm sorry but...'. When people say *with respect*, in fact they mean the opposite.

Audiences are tuned to pick up the weasel words of politicians and they can usually see through the arrogance of managers who use them at work. Many in a senior position in a large company have used terms originated in a political setting.

Weasel words are so ingrained in our corporate psyche that it's going to be difficult to rid ourselves of them, but go they must!

16

And Finally…

'English grammar is so complex and
confusing for the one very simple reason
that its rules and terminology are based
on Latin – a language with which it has
precious little in common.'

Bill Bryson

It's easy to get confused about English and how to use it; it's endlessly adaptable, its rules are open to abuse and as a 'magpie' language it borrows heavily. Without getting too heavy about it, here are some rules (axioms!) to help you improve your style and enable you to get your point across effectively.

1. It's important to prepare properly: rehearse speeches and presentations, and re-write and proofread important documents. Sloppy work is ignored.

2. Be aware of your audience, who they are and what is acceptable. Keep checking to ensure they are listening. Listen to them.

3. Keep it simple; it's a cliché but don't be tempted to over-elaborate just to look clever. Be clear and succinct, especially when presenting – slides should have no more than four bullet points and one picture.

4. Avoid ugly words such *got*, *get*, *done*, *had*... Use more elegant words like *received*.

5. It may seem obvious, but it's important to learn the difference between...

   Have, *had* and *has*
   Here and *hear*
   It's (it is) and *its*
   There and *their*
   Where and *were*
   Your and *you're (you are)*

6. Don't over-elaborate sentences. For example *At this point in time I'd just like to point you in the right direction, so that you can gain the benefit of my expertise* should be *Can I help?*

The usual advice is to keep sentences short and to the point as it can avoid misunderstandings. This is a good idea for email, but long reports can be boring and difficult to follow if they consist of just short sentences. Lengthen a proportion of your sentences to add variety and interest.

Long sentences should cover one topic or clause; too many and it becomes confusing. Paragraphs should stick to one subject.

7. It helps to write like you talk; this gives a natural rhythm to your words and makes your message accessible. The exception to this is when corresponding over something formal such as a legal matter.

8. Be precise about meanings. Avoid the following words and phrases:

At the end of the day...
At all (as in *Can I help at all?*)
Best (as in *best practice*)
Early on (it's just *early*)
Environment (as in *the working environment*)
I feel (as in *I feel that...*)
Going forward
Great (as in *a great amount*)
Having said that...

Interesting (as in *it will be interesting to see*)
I think (as in *I think that*)
In the field of...
Mostly (as in *mostly good*)
Off of (it's just *off*)
Really (as in *really interesting*)
Things (as in *things will improve*)
Wonderful (as in *wonderful scenario*)

9. Avoid vagueness and especially diplomat-speak. I once received the following note:

> In hindsight, it was felt that your performance could be interpreted as sub-optimal. There is the possibility that you may not have been on the top of your game due to over extension; with this in mind it occurs to us that going forward, your preparation could be improved by the addition and aid of one experienced full-time equivalent. We hope that this will ameliorate the situation.

What they really meant was:

> You weren't properly prepared so missed the target, but we accept that you're short staffed. To help you hit the next target we'll increase your team by one.

10. Avoid writing to impress. Using overly complex terms or long words for the sake of it destroys credibility and the reader switches off.

11. Jargon should be avoided; however, it is acceptable if your audience is familiar with the terminology.

12. Get a good dictionary. Some people get surprisingly annoyed at sloppy spelling and they're useful for checking pronunciation too.

13. There are some key differences between British and American English spelling, as illustrated in the table below.

British	**American**
-ence *(defence)*	-ense *(defense)*
-ise *(recognise)*	-ize *(recognize)*
-ogue *(dialogue)*	-og *(dialog)*
-our *(honour)*	-or *(honor)*
-re *(centre)*	-er *(center)*

American spelling sometimes does not have two consonants at the end of a word, while British spelling does, especially when the consonant is an 'l'. For example, the British spellings for *travel*, *traveller*, *travelling* converts to the US *travel*, *traveler* and *traveling*.

Let's conclude with a final list of weasel words:

Connect – to talk, make contact. 'We must connect with our customers' or 'I'm not feeling any connection with you' are generally used by people who have no clue how to communicate properly and are usually mystified by the fact that others don't agree with their point of view. Using the word in conversation signifies the most desperate and least socially adjusted of your colleagues. They are to be avoided, disconnected in fact.

Empathy – a word usually used to indicate that the

158

company is on the customer's side, being aware of their needs in a sympathetic and thoughtful way. In this context it has become a euphemism covering the process whereby companies fake empathy with the customer so that they become loyal spenders, leading to bigger profits.

Focus – to be a centre of attention or an activity, *in the spotlight*, or *under the lens*. A true classic, nearly all managers have used the word, mainly when they think their teams have taken their *eyes off the ball* and won't be *on the A-game*. We get *customer focused*, *team focused*, *client focused*, *career focused* and on and on – well, this book is bad-language focused – and the word should be banned.

Going forward – surely one of the most overused and meaningless political clichés. This phrase has in recent years spread like a virus with no apparent antidote. Businesspeople, politicians, reporters use it freely without restraint – after all, what other direction could they possibly go?

Holistic – to take in the whole picture. A classic bit of consultant bullshit where they talk about taking a holistic approach, encompassing all aspects of a problem because that will give the best results. It will also take the most time and make the consultant more money as a consequence.

Scope, *scoping the opportunity* – range, size, how much profit is there? Another from the consultant's handbook – the bigger the scope of the job, the bigger the contract, the more money made.

Synergy – cooperative interaction among the departments or merged parts of a company that creates something stronger and works to better effect. One of the classic business guru words; forgetting the *human factor*, they dream of organisations, corporations and governments working in harmony to solve problems: with synergy world famine could be eradicated, disease wiped out, war banished and global warming a thing of the past...

These last few terms represent those that have become synonymous with bad language in business as their original meanings have become corrupted by misuse and overuse. Companies should consider language training, particularly for key members who must communicate effectively with potential clients and customers. It is also important for internal communications. It reduces the likelihood of errors, helps create a more harmonious workplace and ensures that everyone knows and understands how the business functions. Credibility is of utmost importance in business and language, and the way we use language is crucial in building, strengthening and maintaining business relationships.